# Cambridge Direct Mathematics

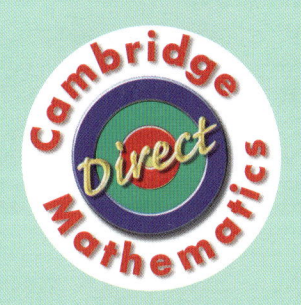

## Pupil's Textbook

### 2

PUBLISHED BY THE PRESS SYNDICATE OF THE UNIVERSITY OF CAMBRIDGE
The Pitt Building, Trumpington Street, Cambridge, United Kingdom

CAMBRIDGE UNIVERSITY PRESS
The Edinburgh Building, Cambridge CB2 2RU, UK
40 West 20th Street, New York, NY 10011-4211, USA
477 Williamstown Road, Port Melbourne, VIC 3207, Australia
Ruiz de Alarcón 13, 28014 Madrid, Spain
Dock House, The Waterfront, Cape Town 8001, South Africa

http://www.cambridge.org

© Cambridge University Press 2002

First published 2002

Printed in the United Kingdom at the University Press, Cambridge

*Typefaces* Frutiger, Helvetica, Minion Swift   *System* QuarkXPress® 4.03

*A catalogue record for this book is available from the British Library*

ISBN 0 521 01165 5 paperback

Text illustration by Bethan Matthews, Liane Payne

Project management by Cambridge Publishing Management

**Main author** for *Cambridge Mathematics Direct at Key Stage One*
Jeanette Mumford

**Contributors** to *Pupil's Textbook 2*
Pete Crawford, Kate Grafham, Claire Grigson, Sue Hood, Kerry Lundy, Julie Moulsdale, Jeanette Mumford, Kathryn Slowey, Allison Toogood, Elizabeth Toohig, Joanne Woodward

The writers and publishers would like to thank the many schools and individuals who trialled lessons for Cambridge Mathematics Direct.

NOTICE TO TEACHERS
It is illegal to reproduce any part of this work in material form
(including photocopying and electronic storage)
except under the following circumstances:
(i) where you are abiding by a licence granted to your school or institution by
the Copyright Licensing Agency;
(ii) where no such licence exists, or where you wish to exceed the terms of
a licence, and you have gained the written permission of
Cambridge University Press;
(iii) where you are allowed to reproduce without permission under
the provisions of Chapter 3 of the Copyright, Designs and Patents Act 1988.

## Abbreviations and symbols

IP is Interactive Picture

AS is Activity Sheet

A is practice work

B develops ideas

C is extension work

★ if needed, helps with work in A

A red margin indicates that children work with the teacher.

A green margin indicates that children work independently.

# Contents

## Numbers and the Number System

### Numbers (N): Counting, properties of numbers and number sequences
| | | |
|---|---|---|
| **N3.3** | Odd and even puzzles | 5 |
| **N4.4** | Investigating steps of 2 | 6 |
| **N4.5** | Solving puzzles and problems | 7 |
| **N5.1** | Steps of 5 | 8 |
| **N5.3** | Multiples of 5 | 9 |
| **N6.2** | Continuing sequences | 10 |
| **N6.3** | Patterns and predictions | 11 |
| **N6.4** | Extending puzzles | 12 |

### Place value (PV): Place value and ordering
| | | |
|---|---|---|
| **PV2.4** | More ordering | 13 |
| **PV2.6** | 1p or 10p more or less | 14 |
| **PV3.2** | Numbers between | 15 |
| **PV3.4** | 100 square jigsaws | 16 |
| **PV3.5** | Number patterns | 17 |

### Estimating and rounding (E)
| | | |
|---|---|---|
| **E1.3** | Rounding to the nearest 10 | 18 |

### Fractions (F)
| | | |
|---|---|---|
| **F2.2** | Fractions of a set | 19 |
| **F2.3** | Half of a number | 20 |
| **F3.1** | Making one whole | 21 |
| **F3.3** | Halves on a number line | 22 |

## Calculations

### Addition and subtraction (AS)
| | | |
|---|---|---|
| **AS3.3** | Adding and subtracting multiples of 10 and 100 | 24 |
| **AS4.4** | Adding 9 or 11 by adjusting | 26 |
| **AS5.1** | Adding and subtracting single digits | 28 |
| **AS5.2** | Adding 2-digit numbers to multiples of 10 | 29 |
| **AS6.2** | Recording pounds and pence | 30 |
| **AS6.3** | Money problems | 31 |
| **AS7.1** | Subtraction as difference | 32 |
| **AS7.4** | Adding or subtracting multiples of 10 | 34 |
| **AS8.1** | Bridging through 10 | 35 |
| **AS8.2** | Partitioning into tens and units | 36 |
| **AS8.3** | Adding and subtracting a 'teens' number | 37 |
| **AS9.2** | Using near doubles | 38 |
| **AS9.3** | Doubling multiples of 5 | 39 |

### Multiplication and division (MD)

| | | |
|---|---|---|
| **MD2.4** | Using symbols | 40 |
| **MD2.5** | Multiplying situations | 41 |
| **MD3.3** | Halving large numbers | 42 |
| **MD3.4** | Undoing halving | 43 |
| **MD4.3** | Grouping | 44 |
| **MD4.4** | Sharing and grouping problems | 45 |
| **MD5.2** | Using place value to divide | 46 |
| **MD5.3** | Multiplying by 2, 3, 4 or 5 | 48 |
| **MD5.4** | Solving multiplication and division problems | 49 |

### Solving problems (SP)

| | | |
|---|---|---|
| **SP2.2** | Add, subtract, multiply or divide | 50 |
| **SP2.3** | Using more than 1 operation | 51 |
| **SP3.1** | Using addition and subtraction | 52 |
| **SP3.2** | Missing numbers | 53 |
| **SP3.3** | Choosing operations | 54 |

# Measures, Shape, Space and Handling Data

### Measures (M)

| | | |
|---|---|---|
| **M4.3** | Solving weight problems | 55 |
| **M6.2** | Multiplying and dividing capacities | 57 |
| **M6.3** | Solving capacity problems | 58 |
| **M7.4** | Quarter to | 59 |
| **M7.6** | Time problems 2 | 60 |

### Shape and space (SS)

| | | |
|---|---|---|
| **SS2.4** | Solving shape problems | 61 |
| **SS3.2** | A line of symmetry | 62 |
| **SS3.3** | Making symmetrical patterns | 63 |
| **SS4.1** | Where is it? | 64 |
| **SS4.2** | Routes | 65 |
| **SS4.3** | Clockwise or anti-clockwise? | 66 |
| **SS5.1** | Right angles | 67 |
| **SS5.2** | Moving shapes | 68 |

### Handling data (HD)

| | | |
|---|---|---|
| **HD2.2** | Reading pictograms | 69 |
| **HD3.1** | Block graphs | 71 |
| **HD3.2** | Reading block graphs | 72 |

# N3.3 Odd and even puzzles

> **Key idea** — We can solve problems and ask questions about odd and even numbers.

**B1** You need a copy of AS 19 and scissors OR a set of dominoes.

This domino has an odd total of spots.

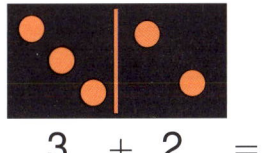

3 + 2 = 5

Find and draw a domino for each of these odd totals of spots.

**a** 3    **b** 7    **c** 9    **d** 11

**B2** Copy each triangle.

Write an odd number in each circle. The 3 odd numbers must add to make the number in the middle.

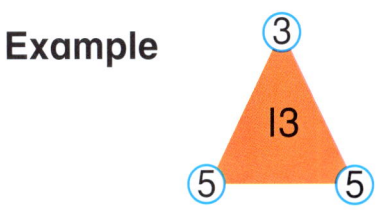

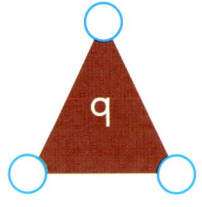

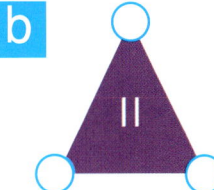

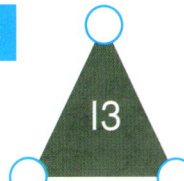

**Example**: 13 (with 3, 5, 5)

**a** 9    **b** 11    **c** 13    **d** 15

**B3**

**a** I have three coins in my purse.

The highest is 10p.
If the other 2 coins are even, how much money do I have?

**b** What if … both coins are odd? How much money might I have?

**C1** Write another 'What if …?' question about the 3 coins in the purse. The highest is 10p. Then work out the answer.

*There may be more than one answer that works.*

N3 Odds and evens

# N4.4 Investigating steps of 2

> **Key idea**  We can discover number patterns ourselves.

Use the staircase.

**B1**  Make 5 steps of 2.

**a**

| Start at | Up 5 steps of 2 | Finish at |
|---|---|---|
| 8 | → | 18 |
| 12 | → | ☐ |
| 16 | → | ☐ |
| 20 | → | ☐ |
| 24 | → | ☐ |

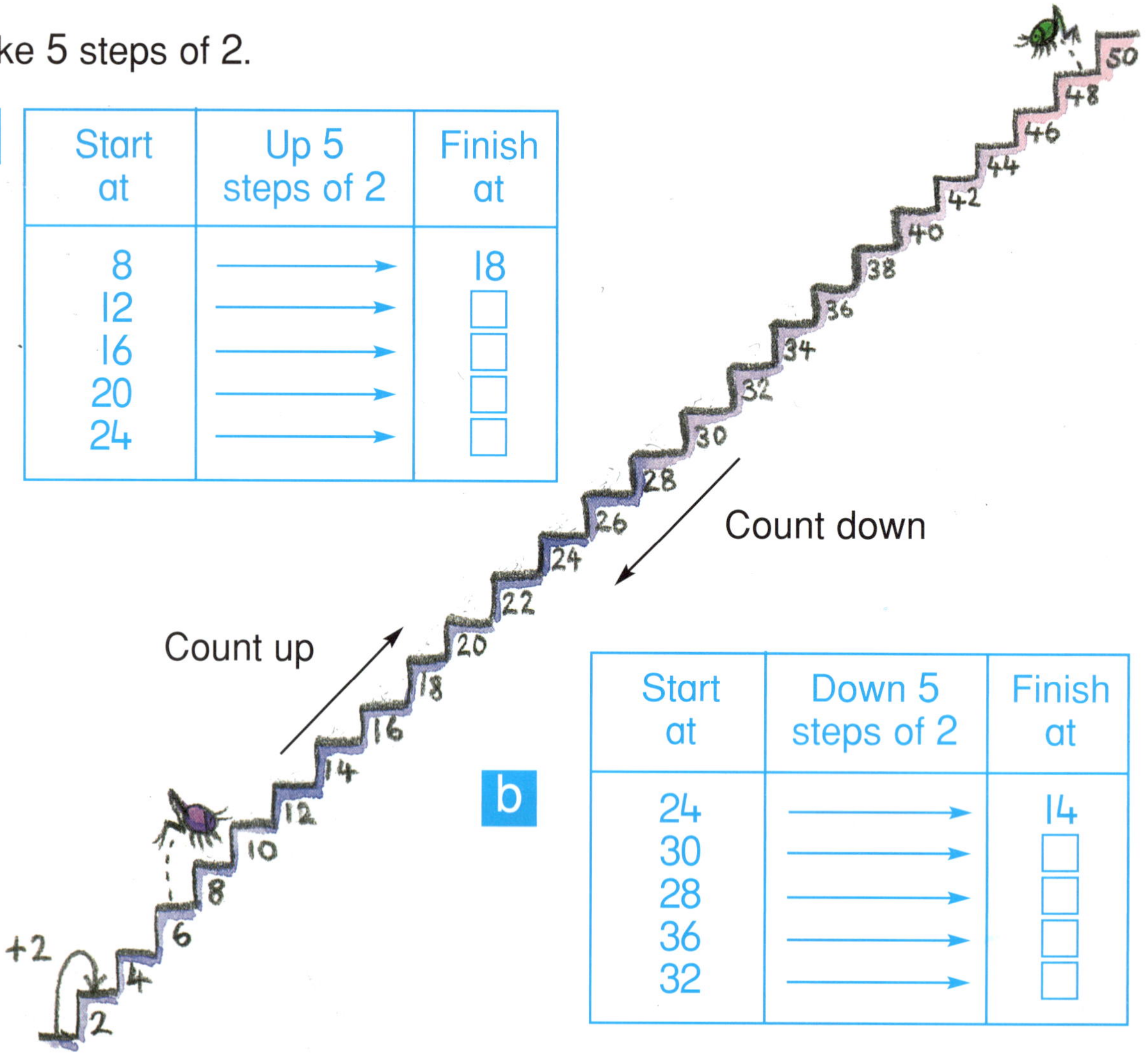

Count up

Count down

**b**

| Start at | Down 5 steps of 2 | Finish at |
|---|---|---|
| 24 | → | 14 |
| 30 | → | ☐ |
| 28 | → | ☐ |
| 36 | → | ☐ |
| 32 | → | ☐ |

**B2**  **a**  Make 10 steps of 2 up the stairs. Start at 6, then 14, then 28.

**b**  Make 10 steps of 2 down the stairs. Start at 48, then 32, then 26.

Record your start and finish numbers.

**B3**  Did you discover any number patterns in B1 and B2? Write about them.

**C1**  Investigate making 20 steps of 2 starting at numbers less than 12.

# N4.5 Solving puzzles and problems

| Key idea | We can use what we know about odd and even numbers to solve problems. |
|---|---|

**Target totals**

**A1** Look at the total score in the centre.

Arrows hitting yellow score 'odd'. Arrows hitting purple score 'even'.

Example: odd, even, 10, 3

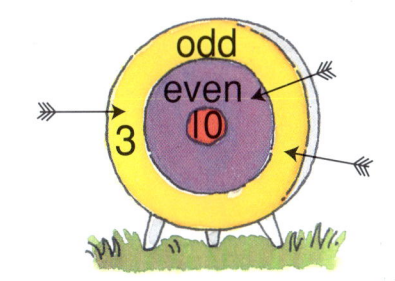

Record 3 + 5 + 2 = 10

Find arrow scores to make the total.

a) 5, 10

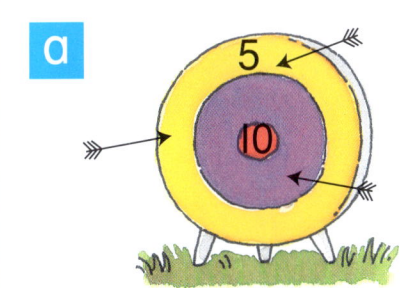

b) 2, 10

c) 10

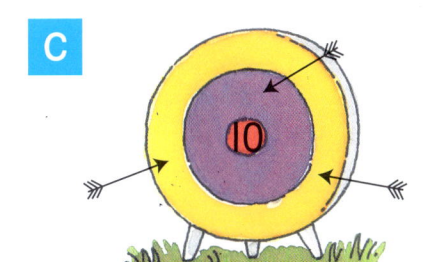

**B1** Do the same as in A1 for these targets.

Find more than 1 way each time.

a) 6

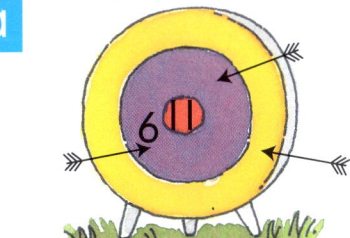

b) 7, 11

c) 11

d) 12

e) 13

f) 14

N4 Steps of 2

7

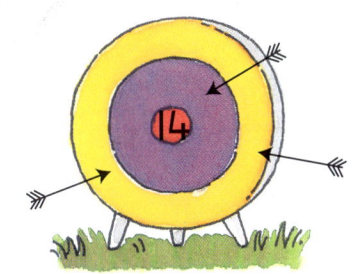

**N5.1** **Steps of 5**

> Key idea — We can count in steps of 5.

★1 **You need digit cards 0–5 and cubes.**

Play 'Count 5s':

- Turn up a card.
- Take cubes to match.
- Put a cube on each dot in this picture.
- Swap over.

No more dots? Make a tower of 5 cubes.

No more cards? Shuffle and use again.

6 towers? You are the winner!

B1 Count in 5s.

There are ☐ brushes altogether.

B2 Copy these sequences. Fill in the missing numbers.

a 5, 10, ☐, ☐, ☐, ☐, 35, ☐, ☐, ☐

b 50, 45, 40, ☐, 30, ☐, ☐

B3 

Make 3 sequences in steps of 5.
Choose starting numbers between 0 and 5.

N5 Counting in 5s

# N5.3 Multiples of 5

> **Key idea** — The units digit of a number tells us whether it is a multiple of 5 or not.

You need some rods and a partner.

## House building

You need 5 rods to build the 1st house.

You need 10 rods to build the 2nd house.

You need 15 rods to build the 3rd house.

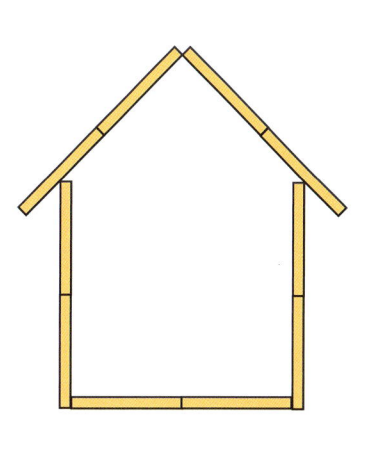

**C1** Work with your partner.
Use your rods to build the 4th and 5th houses.

**C2** Copy and complete this table.

| house | number of rods |
|---|---|
| 1st | 5 |
| 2nd | ☐ |
| 3rd | ☐ |
| 4th | ☐ |
| 5th | ☐ |

**C3** How many rods do you need for:

a  the 6th house?

b  the 8th house?

c  the 10th house?

*Don't build them! Use your table to help.*

N5 Counting in 5s

# N6.2 Continuing sequences

> **Key idea** Number patterns change when we use a different grid.

You need AS 33 and coloured pencils.

**A1** Jump on in 3s from 1 on:

a grid **1**   b grid **2**

**A2** Describe the patterns in A1.

**A3** Jump on in 4s from 1 on grid **3**.

**A4** a Jump on in 3s from 3 on grid **4**.

b Jump on in 4s from 4 on grid **6**.

**B1** Jump on in 3s from 2 on

a grid **5**   b grid **6**

**B2** Describe the patterns in B1.

**B3** a Jump back in 3s from 36 on grid **2**.

b Jump back in 4s from 36 on grid **4**.

**B4** Which numbers are in both patterns on grid **2** and grid **4**?

*Choose a different colour for each question.*

**B5** Investigate jumps of 4 on grids **1** and **3**. Choose your own starting number.

**C** You need AS 34 and a partner.
Play 'Star-gazing':

Count on 4   25   29

N6 Patterns and sequences

# N6.3 Patterns and predictions

> **Key idea** | A pattern can help us predict the answer to a problem.

## Windmills

You need some cubes.

**C1**
- **a** Build the sails of the first windmill with 5 cubes.
  Add different coloured cubes for each new set of sails.
- **b** Add on some more cubes to make the second set of sails.
- **c** Add on some more cubes again to make the third set of sails.

The wind turns the sails of a windmill.

**C2** In the same way, make the next two pairs of sails in the pattern.

**C3** Predict how many cubes you will need for the sixth set of sails.

**C4** Copy and complete this table:

| windmill sails | 1st | 2nd | 3rd | 4th | 5th | 6th |
|---|---|---|---|---|---|---|
| number of cubes | 5 | ☐ | ☐ | ☐ | ☐ | ☐ |

**C5** How many cubes will you need to build the 10th windmill?

N6 Patterns and sequences

# N6.4 Extending puzzles

> **Key idea**: We can investigate a puzzle when we ask 'What if ...?'

## A  Cat collection

You need AS 36 and scissors.

**A1** Cut out the 2 heads, the 2 bodies and the 2 tails.

This is a number 8 cat because 5 + 4 − 1 = 8

**A2** Make as many different cats as you can.

Record their numbers.

**A3** What if ... you change the number on the body to 6?

Can you make more different kinds of cat?

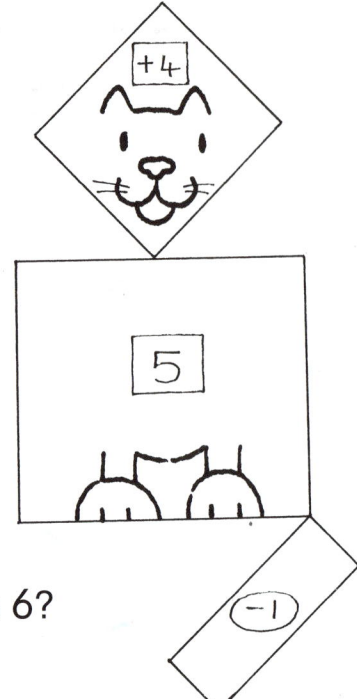

## B1  Cat snacks

Put 15 cat snacks on 3 dishes so that each dish has 3 more snacks than the one before.

Write how many snacks each cat gets.

**B2** What if ... you have 18 cat snacks?

How many snacks will each cat get?

**B3** What if ... you have 21 snacks?

What will each cat get?

N6 Patterns and sequences

## PV2.4 More ordering

> **Key idea**: When we order 2-digit numbers we look first at the tens digit and then at the units digit.

**B1** Look at the numbers on the two outside houses.
The middle house number is halfway between them.
Find the number of each middle house.

a) 22, __, 28

b) 36, __, 46

c) 57, __, 63

d) 83, __, 89

**B2** Order these letters. Begin with the largest number each time.

a) 28, 17, 86, 73, 53

b) 41, 36, 60, 92, 46

**C1** Find the missing numbers. The number halfway between is on the middle house.

a) 16, 22, __

b) __, 47, 54

**C2** Make up missing number puzzles for your partner to solve.
Use 'halfway between' numbers.

PV2 Exploring place value

**PV2.6** # 1p or 10p more or less

| Key idea | We can use what we know about place value to help us solve problems. |

**B1** Work out how much money each child has saved.

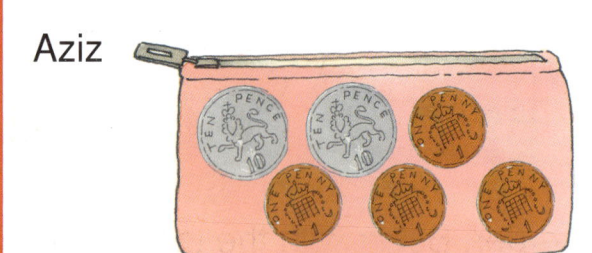

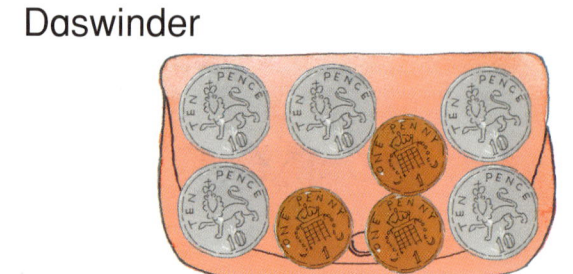

Aziz

Bianca

Cleo

Daswinder

**B2** Use your answers to B1 to solve these:

**a** Who has saved 10p more than Aziz?

**b** Who has saved 10p less than Daswinder?

**c** Amy saved 10p more than Bianca. How much did Amy save?

**d** Daswinder has saved 10p less than Peter. How much has Peter saved?

**C1** Use your answers to B1 to solve these.

**a** How much more has Cleo saved than Bianca?

**b** How much more has Daswinder saved than Aziz?

Use what you know about place value.

**C2** Make up your own problems for your partner to solve.

14

PV2 Exploring place value

## PV3.2 Numbers between

> **Key idea**: A number lying between two numbers is greater than the first number and smaller than the second number.

**B1**
a  Write the shirt numbers in order. Begin with the smallest number.

  54   48   45   52   43

b  Write the shorts numbers in order. Begin with the largest number.

  64   75   46   57   68

**B2** Write the even numbers that lie between these numbers.

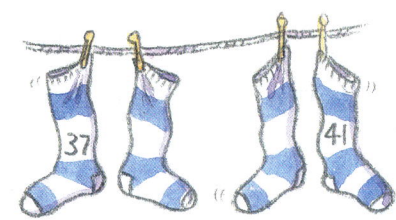

a  24   30

b  37   41

**B3** Write the odd numbers that lie between these numbers.

a  12   19

b  28   42

**C1** Which player scored:
  a  between 25 and 30 goals
  b  between 30 and 35 goals
  c  between 35 and 40 goals
  d  between 45 and 50 goals

Bert 42   Jan 28   Vera 49   Ron 34   Pat 37

PV3 Using place value

# PV3.4 100 square jigsaws

> **Key idea** We can use what we know about place value to find missing numbers.

**B1** Each shape is part of a 100 square.
Find the missing numbers.

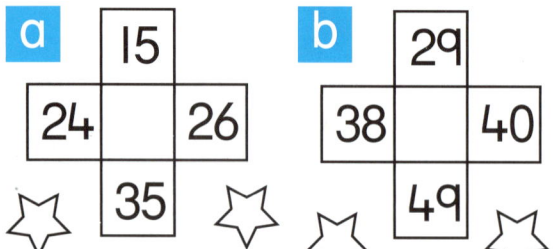

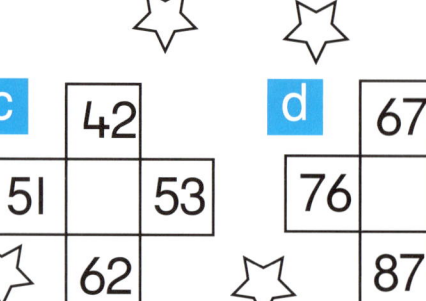

a)
|    | 15 |    |
|----|----|----|
| 24 |    | 26 |
|    | 35 |    |

b)
|    | 29 |    |
|----|----|----|
| 38 |    | 40 |
|    | 49 |    |

c)
|    | 42 |    |
|----|----|----|
| 51 |    | 53 |
|    | 62 |    |

d)
|    | 67 |    |
|----|----|----|
| 76 |    | 78 |
|    | 87 |    |

**B2** These staircases can be found in a 100 square.
Find the missing numbers.

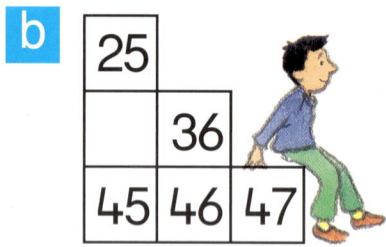

a)
|    |    | 9  |
|----|----|----|
|    |    | 19 |
| 27 | 28 | 29 |

b)
| 25 |    |    |
|----|----|----|
|    | 36 |    |
| 45 | 46 | 47 |

c)
| 42 |    |    |
|----|----|----|
| 52 | 53 |    |
|    | 63 | 64 |

d)
|    |    |     |
|----|----|-----|
|    | 89 | 90  |
| 98 | 99 | 100 |

e)
| 71 |    |    |
|----|----|----|
| 81 | 82 |    |
| 91 |    | 93 |

f)
|    |    | 67 |
|----|----|----|
|    |    | 77 |
| 85 | 86 | 87 |

**C1** These staircases are different.
Use the clues. Write the numbers in the 4th row.

a)
|    |    | 63 |    |
|----|----|----|----|
|    | 71 | 72 |    |
| 79 | 80 | 81 |    |
|    |    |    |    |

b)
|    |    | 17 |
|----|----|----|
|    | 25 | 26 |
| 33 | 34 | 35 |
|    |    |    |

## PV3.5 Number patterns

| Key idea | We can find patterns when we add 10 to a number. |
|---|---|

**B1** Do B1 on AS 68.

**B2** Copy and complete these potato print patterns.

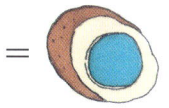

**a**
64 = ◯ + 4
64 = ◯ + 14
64 = ◯ + 24
64 = ◯ + 34

**b**
57 = △ + 7
57 = △ + 17
57 = △ + 27
57 = △ + 37

**c**
85 = 80 + ⬠
85 = 70 + ⬠
85 = 60 + ⬠
85 = 50 + ⬠

**d**
93 = 90 + ◯
93 = 80 + ◯
93 = 70 + ◯
93 = 60 + ◯

**C1** Continue the potato print patterns in B2.
Write the next 2 lines each time.

**C2** Investigate a number between 100 and 110.
Make your own pattern.

PV3 Using place value

AS 68 | 17

# E1.3 Rounding to the nearest 10

| Key idea | Numbers that end in 1, 2, 3 or 4 round down to the 10 before. Numbers that end in 5, 6, 7, 8 or 9 round up to the next 10. |

**A1** Estimate how far each snail has crawled.
Write your answer to the nearest 10.

**B1** Write the nearest tens number for these bags of bulbs.

a  19
b  51
c  32
d  38
e  27
f 43

**B2** Round the number of seedlings in each pot to the nearest 10.

a  31
b  52
c  29
d  15
e  36
f 35

18  E1 Estimating and rounding

# F2.2 Fractions of a set

| Key idea | We can find one quarter of a set. |
|---|---|

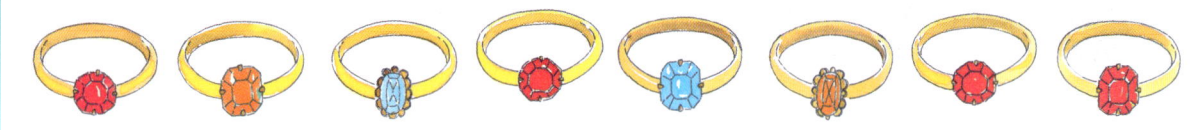

**B1**  Write the fraction of the rings that have:

  a  red rubies
  b  blue sapphires

**B2**  What fraction of these shells have a pearl?

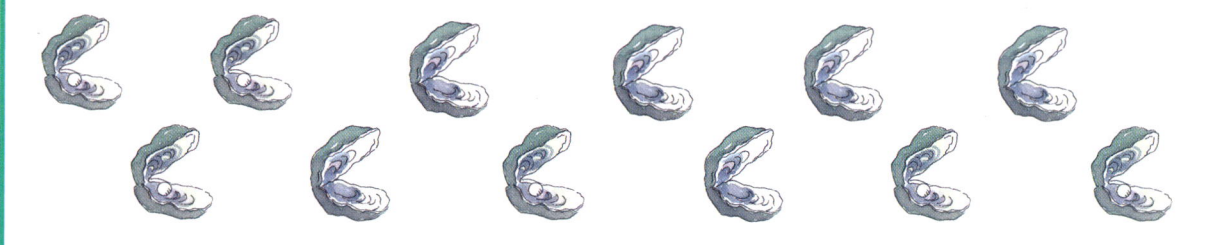

**B3**
- Count the beads on each necklace.
- Write the fraction of the beads that are yellow.

  a 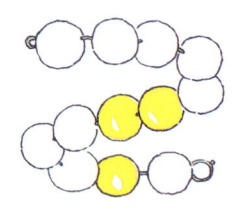
  b 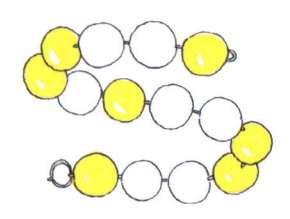
  c 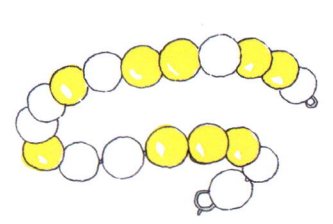
  d

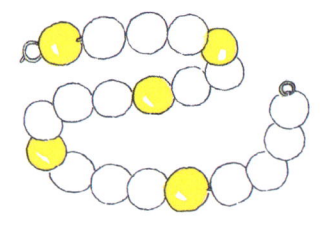

**B4**  Can you find half of these sets of shells? Try to draw 2 equal groups.

  a 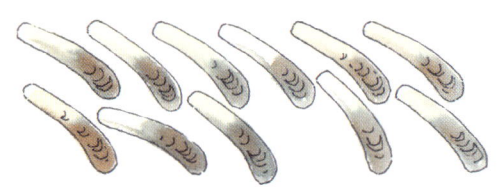
  b

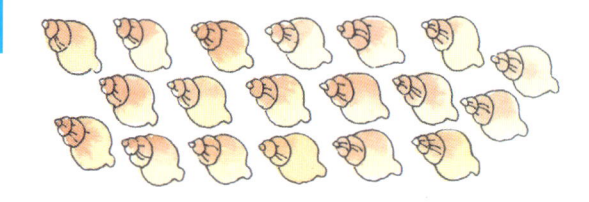

F2 Fractions of a set

## F2.3 Half of a number

> **Key idea**  We can find half of an even number.

**B1**

**a** Half of the ducks go to swim in the pond.
How many ducks go swimming?

**b** These starlings land in a field.
Then 7 fly away.
What fraction are left?

**c** Bruce hides $\frac{1}{4}$ of his bones under an oak tree.
How many bones does he hide?

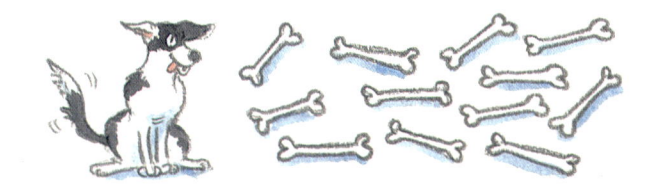

**d** Bruce rounds up the sheep with black faces.
What fraction of the sheep does he round up?

**C1** In a game Derek won half the stickers.

Amy won one quarter and Simon won the rest.

How many stickers does each child get?

**C2** Make up a problem about the sheep in B1 **d**.
Ask a friend to solve it.

20   F2 Fractions of a set

# F3.1 Making one whole

> **Key idea** — Two halves or four quarters make one whole.

**B** Match the halves and quarters to make whole cheeses.
Write the letters that make each whole cheese like this:

*a and m*
$\frac{1}{2}$ and $\frac{1}{2}$ make 1 whole.

F3 Equivalent fractions

# F3.3 Halves on a number line

**Key idea** | Fractions are numbers. We can put them on a number line.

**A1**
- Draw the number line each time.
- Write the halfway number.

a) 1 — 2

b) 5 — 6

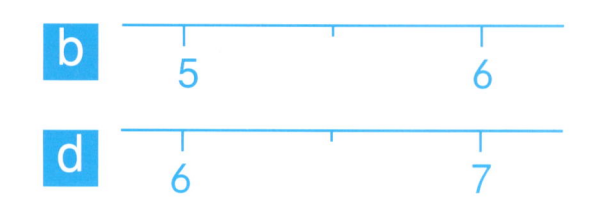

c) 9 — 10

d) 6 — 7

**A2**
- Draw a 0–5 number line.
- Mark all the half numbers.
- Solve these problems. Put each answer on the number line, like this:

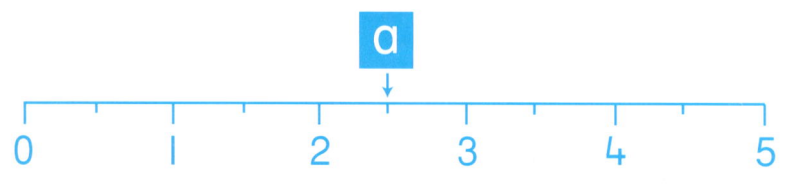

a ↓ 
0 — 1 — 2 — 3 — 4 — 5

a) How many each?

b) How many each?

c) How many each?

d) How many each?

F3 Equivalent fractions

**B1** You need AS 85 and these colours:

Pirate Dan is in a muddle! He has mixed up all the socks.

Socks on number line 0 to 10: 3½, 9½, 5½, 7½, 1½, ½, 8½, 6½, 2½, 4½

- **a** Use AS 85, question B1.
  Write the socks in the correct order and colour them.

- **b** What is the colour of the sock at $5\frac{1}{2}$?

- **c** What numbers mark the pair of red socks?

**B2** Do AS 85, question B2.

**C1** Use AS 85, question C1.
Solve these problems. Put each answer on the number line.

- **a** Share 18 cakes equally between 2 children.

- **b** A piece of string is 15 cm long. How long is one half?

- **c** Sam has 13 biscuits to share with his friend. How many each?

**C2** Write your own fraction problems with answers between 0 and 10.

| Key idea | Fractions are numbers. We can put them on a number line. |

F3 Equivalent fractions

# AS3.3 Adding and subtracting multiples of 10 and 100

> **Key idea** | Learning to add and subtract multiples of 10 and 100.

3p + 1p = 4p   30p + 10p = 40p   300p + 100p = 400p
3  + 1  = 4    30  + 10  = 40    300  + 100  = 400

**A1** Copy and fill in the boxes.

a  2 + 3 = ☐ ⇒ 20 + 30 = ☐ ⇒ 200 + 300 = ☐

b  5 − 4 = ☐ ⇒ 50 − 40 = ☐ ⇒ 500 − 400 = ☐

**A2** Make your own patterns.

*The first pair of numbers must add up to less than 10.*

a  ☐ + ☐ = ☐ ⇒ ☐ + ☐ = ☐ ⇒ ☐ + ☐ = ☐

b  ☐ − ☐ = ☐ ⇒ ☐ − ☐ = ☐ ⇒ ☐ − ☐ = ☐

**A3** Copy and fill in the boxes.

a  60 + 30 = ☐          b  500 + 400 = ☐

c  60 − 40 = ☐          d  700 − 200 = ☐

AS3 Using patterns of calculations

**B1** You need a dice marked with numbers 0, 10, 20, 30, 40, 50.

Roll your dice twice.

Use your numbers to write 2 additions.

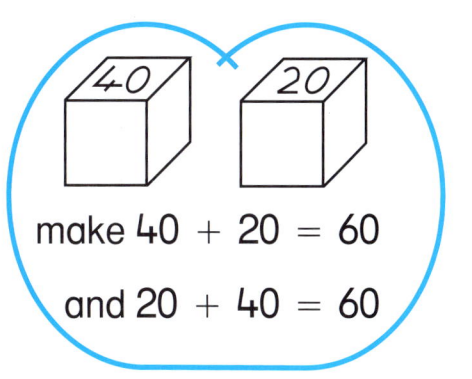

make 40 + 20 = 60

and 20 + 40 = 60

**B2** Now try to write 2 subtractions using the same 3 numbers.

60 − 20 = 40

60 − 40 = 20

**B3** Carry on like this.
Are there any numbers which you can only make 1 subtraction for?

**C1** Copy and fill in the boxes.

a) 20 + ☐ = 50
b) 30 + ☐ = 80
c) ☐ + 40 = 90
d) 200 + ☐ = 700
e) 400 + ☐ = 600
f) ☐ + 300 = 700

**C2** Copy and fill in the boxes.

a) 20 + 70 + 10 = ☐
b) 10 + 60 + 10 = ☐
c) 50 + 30 + 10 = ☐
d) 40 + 30 + 10 = ☐

**C3** How many different ways can you make 700 by adding three multiples of 100?

**Key idea** Learning to add and subtract multiples of 10 and 100.

AS3 Using patterns of calculations

25

# AS4.4 Adding 9 or 11 by adjusting

> **Key idea** We can use adding 10 to help us add 9 or 11.

**A1** Sophie has spilt paint on her work. Was she adding 9 or 11?

a  36 + ⬜ = 45

b  43 + ⬜ = 52

c  61 + ⬜ = 72

d  58 + ⬜ = 67

e  28 + ⬜ = 39

**A2** Draw number lines to show d and e.

Teri aged 9   Fred aged 15   Shanice aged 6   Rashi aged 11   Sam aged 12

**B1** How old will each child be 9 years from now?

**B2** How old will each child be 11 years from now?

**B3** Draw a number line to show how you worked out your answers for Sam.

**C1** You need a dice and number cards.

Choose a card.
Throw the dice.
Write down the addition sentence you can make.

**C2** Draw number lines to show two of your additions.

> **Key idea** We can use adding 10 to help us add 9 or 11.

AS4 Developing mental strategies

27

## AS5.1 Adding and subtracting single digits

> **Key idea** When we add a single digit to a multiple of 10 or 100, only the units digit changes.

Lemonade 90p, Chew 3p, Cola 40p, Spider 8p, Chocolate 30p

**B1** How much do I spend if I buy:
- a) a chocolate bar and a chew?
- b) a can of cola and a spider?
- c) a can of cola and a chew?
- d) a bottle of lemonade and a spider?

**B2** I have a 20p. How much money would I have left if I bought:
- a) a chew?
- b) a spider?

**B3** I buy a pencil.
How much change will I get if I pay with:
- a) 10p?
- b) 20p?
- c) 50p?

Pencil 7p

**B4** Copy and complete.
- a) 100 + 5 = ☐
- b) 2 + 400 = ☐
- c) 500 + 7 = ☐
- d) 8 + 900 = ☐

AS5 Further mental strategies

# AS5.2 Adding 2-digit numbers to multiples of 10

> **Key idea** When we add a 2-digit number and a multiple of 10, the units digit of the answer is the same as the units digit of the 2-digit number.

**B1** How much money do these pairs of children have altogether?

- **a** Elsa and Imam
- **b** Imam and Jason
- **c** Elsa and Jason

**B2** How much more do these children need to save to have 70p?

- **a** Jason
- **b** Elsa

**B3** How much do I spend if I buy:

- **a** a magazine and a pencil?
- **b** a pencil and a pencil sharpener?
- **c** a newspaper and a pencil?
- **d** a newspaper and a magazine?

AS5 Further mental strategies

## AS6.2 Recording pounds and pence

> **Key idea** We can find different ways to pay.

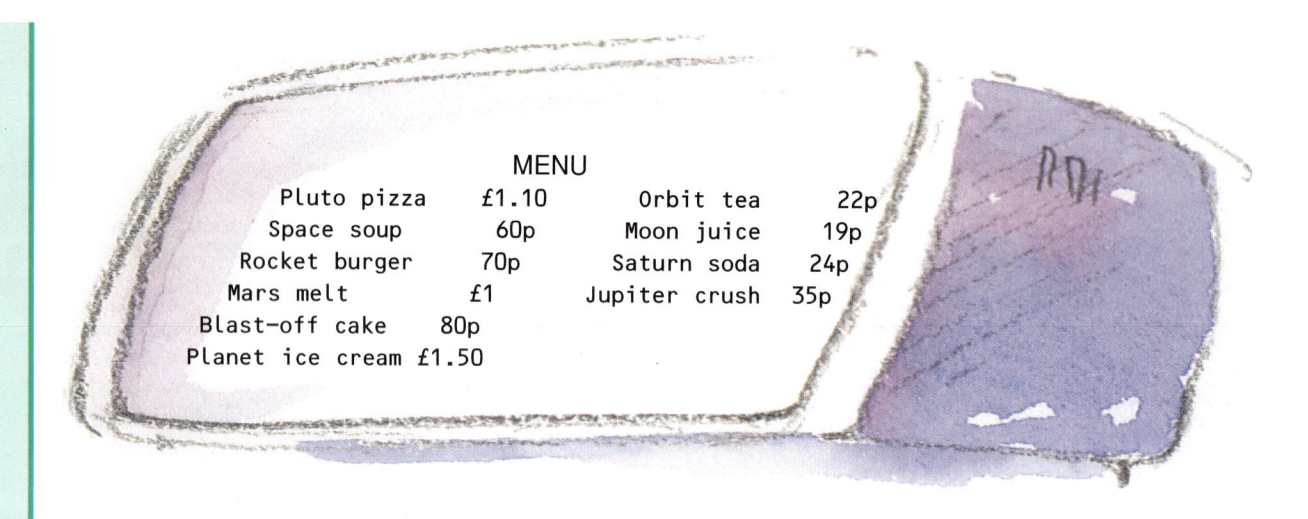

**MENU**

| | | | |
|---|---|---|---|
| Pluto pizza | £1.10 | Orbit tea | 22p |
| Space soup | 60p | Moon juice | 19p |
| Rocket burger | 70p | Saturn soda | 24p |
| Mars melt | £1 | Jupiter crush | 35p |
| Blast-off cake | 80p | | |
| Planet ice cream | £1.50 | | |

**A1** How much did Space Slug pay if he bought:

a. a burger and tea?
b. a cake and juice?
c. soup and soda?
d. a burger and soda?

**A2** Write down 2 different ways to make each total using coins.

**A3** How much do these cost altogether?

a. A Mars melt and juice
b. A Mars melt and soda
c. A Mars melt and crush

**C1** Find the total cost if Space Slug bought:

a. soup and a pizza
b. a burger and a Mars melt
c. ice cream and juice
d. soup, a Mars melt and soda
e. a pizza and ice cream

**C2** Write 2 different ways to make each total using coins.

30    AS6 Money

# AS6.3 Money problems

> **Key idea** We can find totals and give change.

**B1** I have 48p. Can I buy the biscuits and the chocolate?

**B2** Sara buys 2 packs of sweets. One costs 19p and the other costs 28p. She pays with a £1 coin. Which coins might she get as her change?

**B3** Mum has 70p. She buys 3 pencils. How much money has she left?

**B4** Fazir buys a robot and a toy car.

  **a** How much change does he get from £1?

  **b** Which coins can he have in his change?

**B5** I buy 2 drinks and 3 chocolate bars.

  **a** How much do I spend altogether?

  **b** I had £2 to begin with. How much do I have left?

**C** Make up your own word problems about money and find the answers. Use the words total and change.

# AS7.1 Subtraction as difference

> **Key idea** We can use counting on to find the difference between 2 numbers.

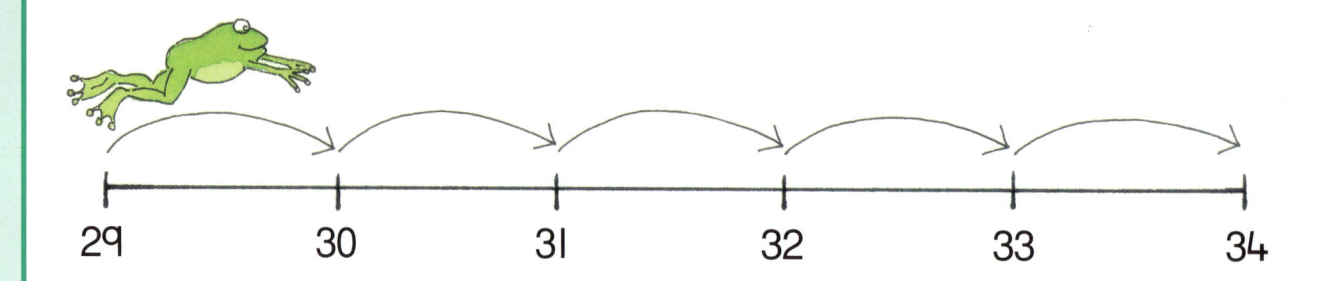

34 − 29 = 5

29  30  31  32  33  34

**A1** Find these differences.

a  33 − 28
b  42 − 36
c  81 − 77
d  65 − 59
e  74 − 68
f  22 − 18
g  52 − 45
h  64 − 57

**B1** 29 − [22] = 7

Here are some differences.
What are the missing numbers?

a  31 − ☐ = 5
b  59 − ☐ = 3
c  92 − ☐ = 4
d  ☐ − ☐ = 6
e  ☐ − ☐ = 5

**C1** How much taller is Jo's flower than Ann's?

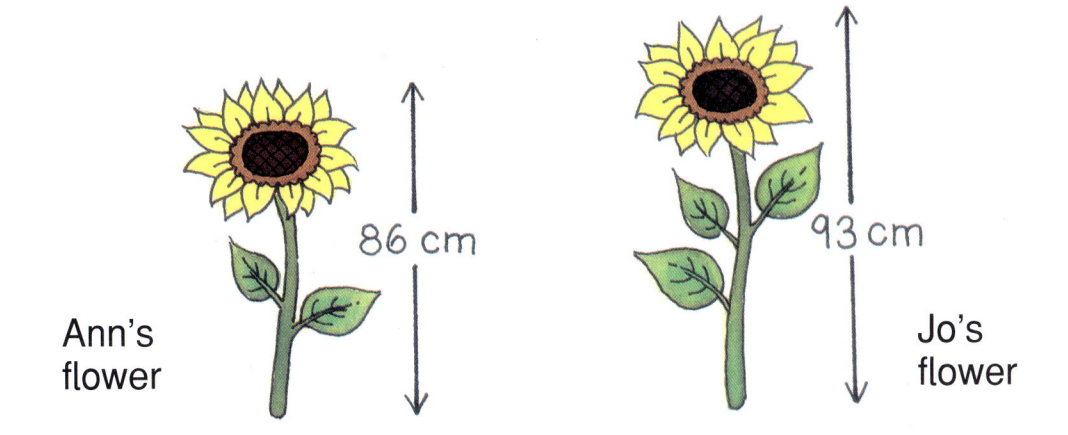

Ann's flower 86 cm

Jo's flower 93 cm

**C2** How much less does the comic cost than the birthday card?

69p

74p

**C3** How much longer is the green snake than the brown one?

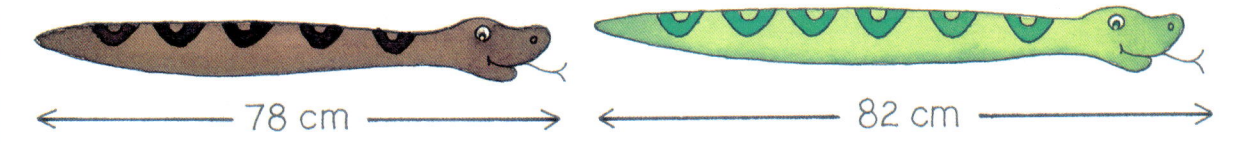

78 cm    82 cm

**C4** What is the difference in cost between the 2 packets of crisps?

27p    31p

**C5** Make up your own word problems about differences and find the answers.

| Key idea | We can use counting on to find the difference between 2 numbers. |

AS7 Difference

# AS7.4 Adding or subtracting multiples of 10

| Key idea | When we add or subtract a multiple of 10 from any 2-digit number, the units digit stays the same. |
|---|---|

**B1**

🐍 + 30 = 64

To find the number Slip the snake is lying on you could do 64 − 30 = 🐍   Answer = 34

Write a subtraction to find the missing numbers.

a  🐍 + 10 = 33

b  🐍 + 40 = 91

c  🐍 + 60 = 82

d  🐍 + 20 = 64

**B2**

🐍 − 20 = 48

To find the number Slip is lying on you could do 48 + 20 = 68

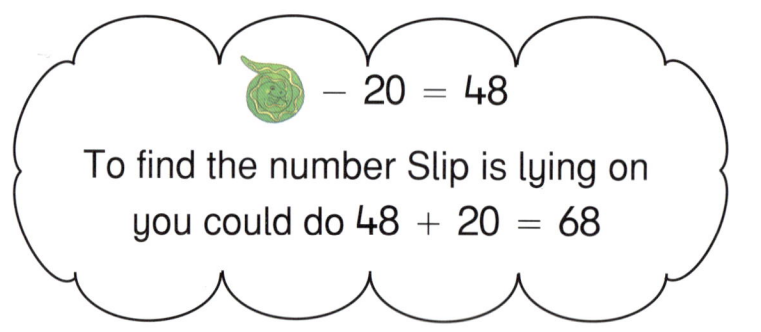

Write an addition to find the missing numbers.

a  🐍 − 10 = 11

b  🐍 − 50 = 44

c  🐍 − 30 = 56

d  🐍 − 20 = 32

**C** Make up your own Slip the snake missing number problems. For each one show the calculation you could use to find the missing number.

27 + 🐍 = 57    57 − 27 = 30

## AS8.1 Bridging through 10

> **Key idea** — We can add and subtract by counting on or back to 10 or 20 first.

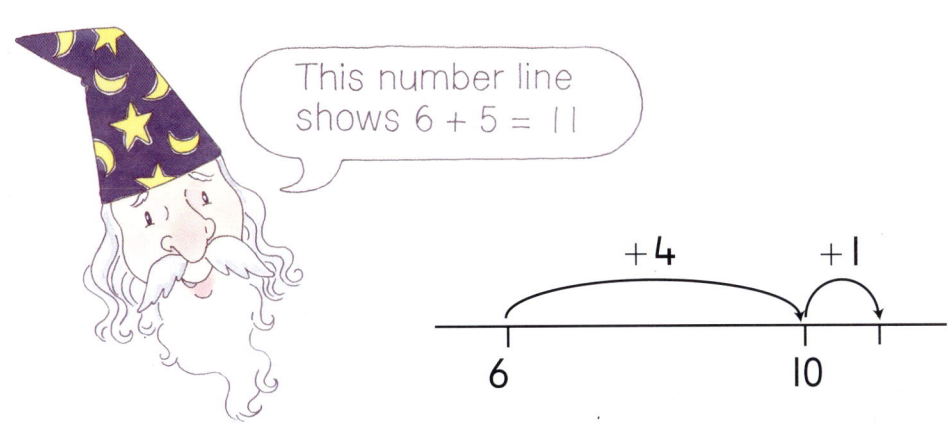

*This number line shows 6 + 5 = 11*

**B1** Write the number sentence shown by each number line.

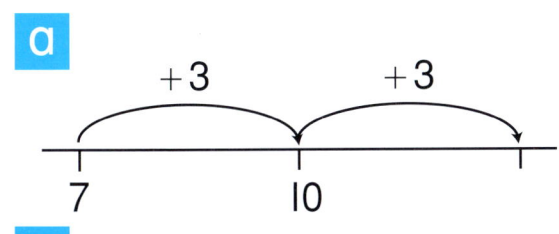

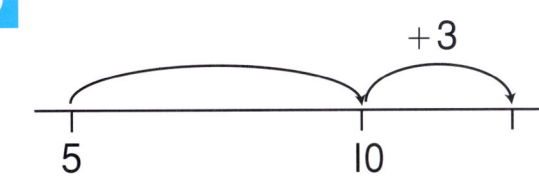

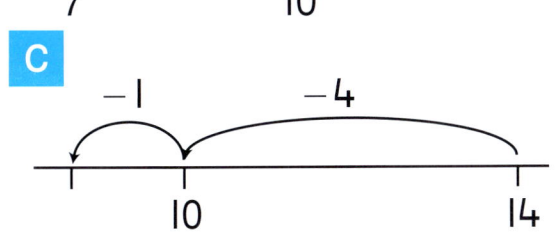

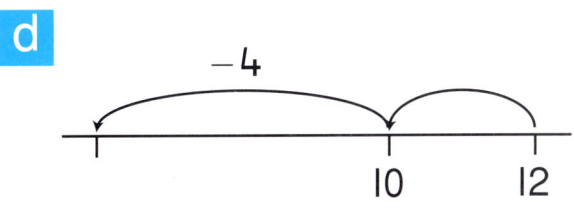

a) 7 ... 10 ... (+3, +3)

b) 5 ... 10 ... (+3)

c) 10 ... 14 ... (−1, −4)

d) 10 ... 12 ... (−4)

**B2** Use counting on or back to 20 first.

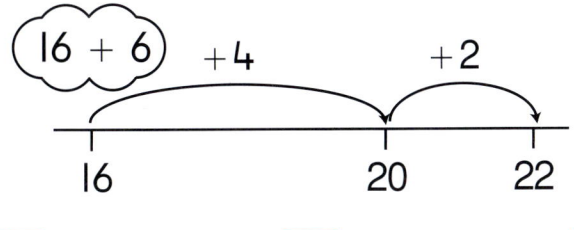

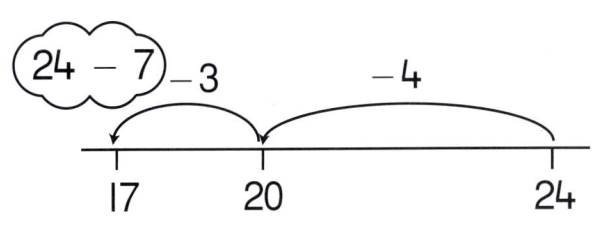

16 + 6: 16 → +4 → 20 → +2 → 22

24 − 7: 24 → −4 → 20 → −3 → 17

a) 17 + 5    b) 14 + 8    c) 22 − 4    d) 25 − 8

**B3** Think of each number as 5 and a bit.

a) 6 + 7    b) 8 + 8
c) 7 + 9    d) 7 + 8

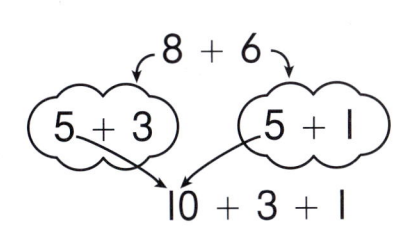

8 + 6 → (5 + 3)(5 + 1) → 10 + 3 + 1

AS8 Partitioning and recombining

## AS8.2 Partitioning into tens and units

**Key idea** — Splitting numbers into tens and units can help us to add.

I can do 23 + 12 by splitting numbers into tens and units.

23 + 12 → 20 + 3, 10 + 2
= (20 + 10) + (3 + 2)
= 30 + 5
= 35

Try these in the same way.

**A1**
a. 15 + 13 = ☐
b. 24 + 14 = ☐
c. 14 + 24 = ☐
d. 26 + 13 = ☐
e. 18 + 21 = ☐
f. 17 + 32 = ☐

Can you work these out in your head? Remember to split each number into tens and units.

**B1**
a. 25 + 24 = ☐
b. 25 + 32 = ☐
c. 36 + 23 = ☐
d. 44 + 33 = ☐
e. 51 + 48 = ☐
f. 52 + 47 = ☐

Use rods and cubes to help you with these.

**B2**
a. 19 + 11 = ☐
b. 27 + 13 = ☐
c. 18 + 2 = ☐
d. 26 + 14 = ☐

AS8 Partitioning and recombining

# AS8.3 Adding and subtracting a 'teens' number

| Key idea | We can add and subtract a 'teens' number to or from a 2-digit number. |

**A1** Use rods and cubes.
Add the ten and then the units.

24 + 13 = ☐ + ☐ = 37

- a  22 + 15
- b  21 + 18
- c  15 + 33
- d  24 + 13
- e  12 + 24
- f  14 + 35

**A2** Use rods and cubes.
Take away the ten and then the units.

25 − 13 = ☐ —−10→ ☐ —−3→ ☐ = 12

- a  34 − 12
- b  28 − 13
- c  25 − 12
- d  48 − 15
- e  27 − 14
- f  32 − 11

**C1** Find the missing numbers
- a  14 + ☐ = 59
- b  ☐ − 17 = 22
- c  ☐ + 15 = 38
- d  ☐ − 13 = 44
- e  13 + ☐ = 87
- f  ☐ − 15 = 54

AS8 Partitioning and recombining

# AS9.2 Using near doubles

| Key idea | Doubles can help us to find near doubles. |

**B1** Find these near doubles.

a  12 + 13 = ☐          b  14 + 15 = ☐

c  11 + 12 = ☐          d  15 + 17 = ☐

*The total cost is 29p. I doubled 14p and then added 1p.*

**B2** What are the total costs? Write a sentence to explain how you worked each one out.

a  apple 13p, cupcake 14p

b  car 15p, boat 16p

c  pencil 12p, 13p

d  banana 16p, Fizzo can 17p

**C1**

Items: red car £15, games console £16, doll £14, box of shapes £13

a  Choose 2 items.
Write down the total cost.
Show how you worked it out.

b  Choose another 2 items.

c  Make up your own near double question.
Ask a friend to solve it.

38  AS9 Doubles

## AS9.3 Doubling multiples of 5

> **Key idea** We can use doubling to help us solve problems.

**B1** Use doubles to find the total cost of each pair.

a) cup 45p, saucer 44p
b) sharpener 26p, pencil 25p
c) cola 35p, choco 36p

**B2** Double the money in each purse.

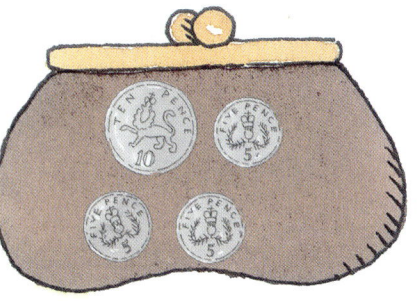

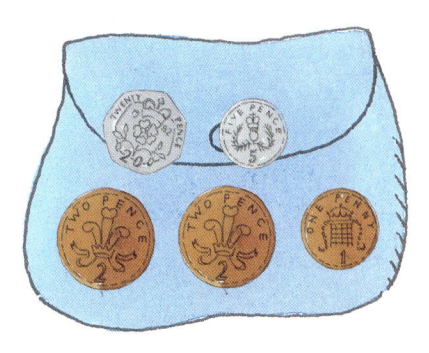

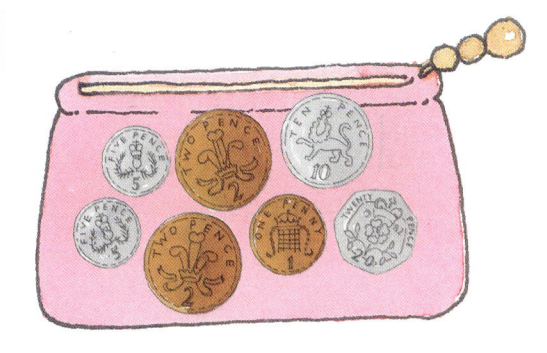

a) 10p, 5p, 2p, 5p
b) 20p, 5p, 2p, 2p, 1p
c) 5p, 1p, 1p, 5p, 1p
d) 5p, 2p, 10p, 2p, 1p, 20p

**C1** Use doubles to find:

a) 25 + 27   b) 50 + 48   c) 30 + 32   d) 19 + 19

**C2** Which doubles did you use?

**C3** Write some near doubles of your own.

AS9 Doubles

39

# MD2.4 Using symbols

| Key idea | Symbols can stand for numbers. |

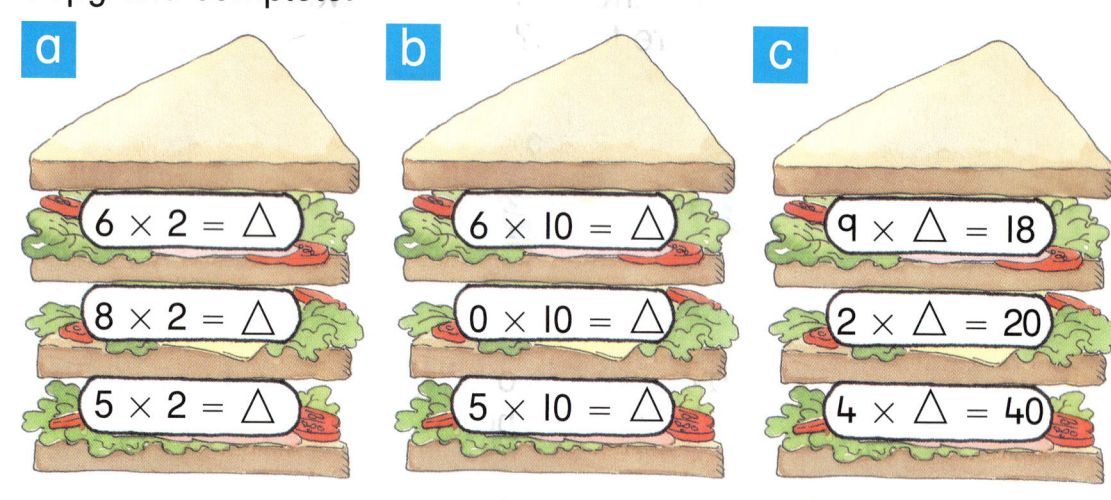

**B1** Copy and complete.

a
- $6 \times 2 = \triangle$
- $8 \times 2 = \triangle$
- $5 \times 2 = \triangle$

b
- $6 \times 10 = \triangle$
- $0 \times 10 = \triangle$
- $5 \times 10 = \triangle$

c
- $9 \times \triangle = 18$
- $2 \times \triangle = 20$
- $4 \times \triangle = 40$

d
- $9 \times \triangle = 90$
- $7 \times \triangle = 14$
- $3 \times \triangle = 6$

e
- $\triangle \times 10 = 0$
- $5 \times \triangle = 50$
- $\triangle \times 7 = 70$

f
- $\triangle \times 4 = 8$
- $\triangle \times 10 = 100$
- $\triangle \times 6 = 12$

**C1** Work out what $\Diamond$ and $\triangle$ could stand for. Copy and complete.

a  $\Diamond \times \triangle = 12$

b  $\Diamond \times \triangle = 18$

c  $\Diamond \times \triangle = 20$

d  $\Diamond \times \triangle = 30$

e  $\Diamond \times \triangle = 22$

f  $\Diamond \times \triangle = 50$

# MD2.5 Multiplying situations

> **Key idea** We can multiply to solve problems.

**B1** There are 2 ponds in the park. There are 4 swans swimming on each pond. How many swans are there?

**B2** Pip and Emma each have 5 slices of bread to feed the ducks. How many slices of bread do they have altogether?

**B3** There are 8 paddle boats on one pond. There are 2 children in each boat. How many children are in the boats?

**B4** There are 4 ducks on the small pond. There are 10 times as many ducks in the large pond. How many ducks are on the large pond?

**B5** Lee and Yan caught 10 fish each. They put the fish in a tank. How many fish were there in the tank?

**B6** There are 10 nests in the trees. There are 5 eggs in each nest. How many eggs are there?

MD2 Arrays

41

# MD3.3 Halving large numbers

> **Key idea** We can find half of a number in many ways.

**A1** Find these halves:
- a) half of 20
- b) half of 50
- c) half of 70
- d) half of 40
- e) half of 30
- f) half of 90

**C1** Complete the question on each train, then find half of each answer.

a) 9 × 2 = ☐    18 ÷ 2 = ☐

b) ☐ × 2 = 16    ☐ ÷ ☐ = ☐

c) ☐ × 2 = 40    ☐ ÷ ☐ = ☐

**C2** Find half of the number on the signal, then write the number sentence.

a) 12 ÷ ☐ = ☐    signal: 12

b) ☐ ÷ ☐ = ☐    signal: 60

c) ☐ ÷ ☐ = ☐    signal: 80

d) ☐ ÷ ☐ = ☐    signal: 14

MD3 Doubling and halving

# MD3.4 Undoing halving

| Key idea | Doubling undoes halving. |
|---|---|

2 rockets land on each planet. Rockets **b** and **g** land on the green planet.

**a** half of 60
**b** double 6
**c** 28 ÷ 2
**d** half of 50
**e** double 15
**f** 90 ÷ 2
**g** half of 24
**h** 100 ÷ 2
**i** 50 ÷ 2
**j** half of 90
**k** double 25
**l** double 7

**B1** Find the pairs of rockets that land on each planet.
Copy and complete the table.

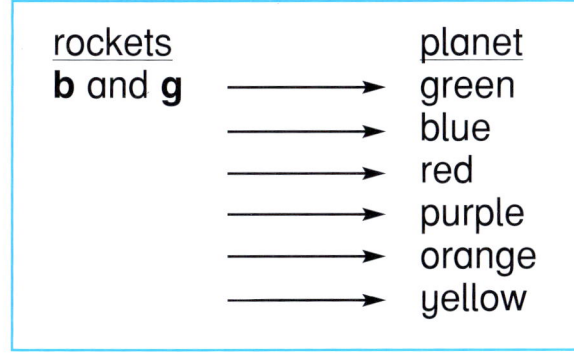

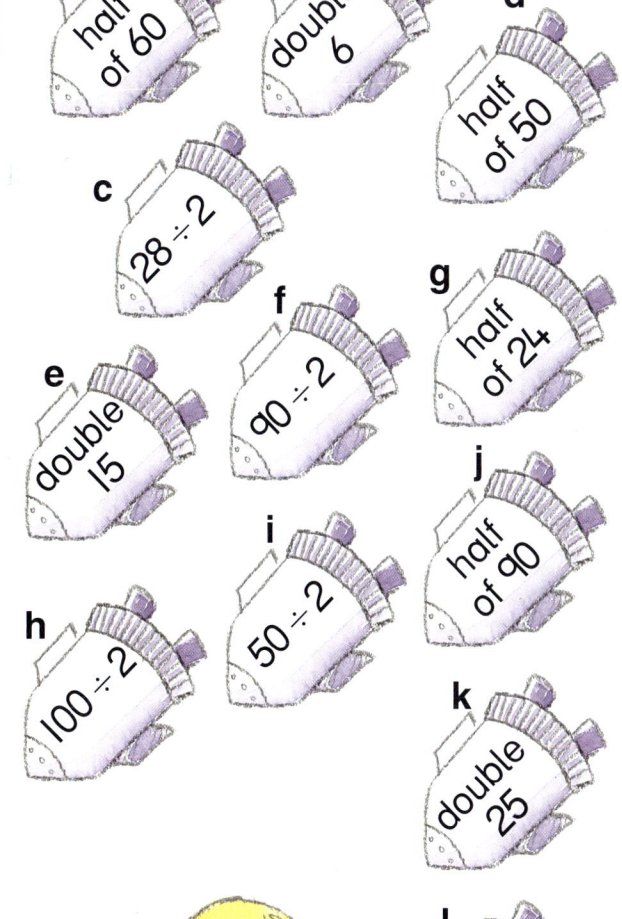

| rockets | planet |
|---|---|
| **b** and **g** → | green |
| → | blue |
| → | red |
| → | purple |
| → | orange |
| → | yellow |

Planets: 12, 14, 30, 50, 25, 45

**C1** Draw pairs of rockets that would land on these planets.

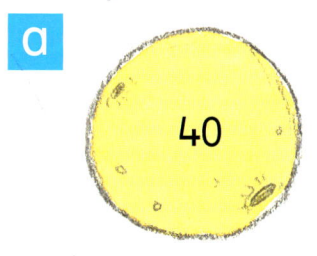

**a** 40   **b** 16   **c** 35

MD3 Doubling and halving

# MD4.3 Grouping

> **Key idea**: We can divide by putting objects into equal groups.

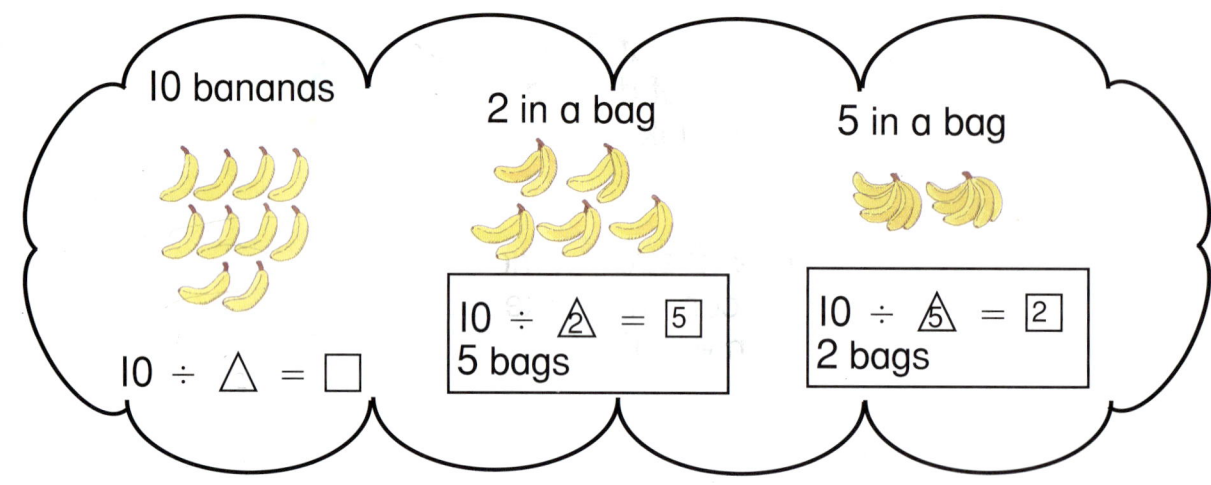

10 bananas

10 ÷ △ = ☐

2 in a bag

10 ÷ △2 = ☐5
5 bags

5 in a bag

10 ÷ △5 = ☐2
2 bags

**B1** Find out how many groups there are and write a number sentence.

14 ÷ △ = ☐
- a  2 in a bunch
- b  7 in a bunch

**B2**

15 ÷ △ = ☐
- a  5 in a bag
- b  3 in a bag

**B3**

20 ÷ △ = ☐
- a  5 on a plate
- b  4 on a plate

**B4**

30 ÷ △ = ☐
- a  10 in a box
- b  3 in a box

## MD4.4 Sharing and grouping problems

| Key idea | We can solve sharing and grouping problems using divided by facts. |

**B1**

**a** There are 15 children at Anne's party.
How many 5-packs of drink are needed if everyone has 1 drink?

**b** Anne's mum has 18 strawberries.
How many tarts can she make with 2 strawberries on each?

**c** They have 20 balloons.
Half are in the hall and the rest in the lounge.
How many are in the lounge?

**d** They made 30 sandwiches and put an equal number on 5 plates.
How many sandwiches are on each plate?

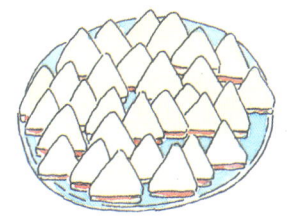

**e** Anne sticks up party streamers.
How many 2 cm lengths can she cut from 10 cm of sticky tape?

**f** Anne's dad has 19 sweets for a treasure hunt.
He hides an equal number in 5 places.
How many does he put in each place?
How many are left over?

**C1** Kumar, Liz, Mark and Nathan shared 10 sausages equally.

Draw pictures to show how they did this.

MD4 Sharing and grouping

45

# MD5.2 Using place value to divide

> **Key idea**: When we divide a multiple of 10 by 10, the tens digit moves to become a units digit.

★1 Write a number sentence for each picture.

a  1 ÷ 1 = 1

b  2 ÷ ☐ = ☐

c  ☐ ÷ ☐ = ☐

d  ☐ ÷ ☐ = ☐

e  ☐ ÷ ☐ = ☐

f  ☐ ÷ ☐ = ☐

g  ☐ ÷ ☐ = ☐

h  ☐ ÷ ☐ = ☐

i  ☐ ÷ ☐ = ☐

j  ☐ ÷ ☐ = ☐

Look what happens when we divide by 1!

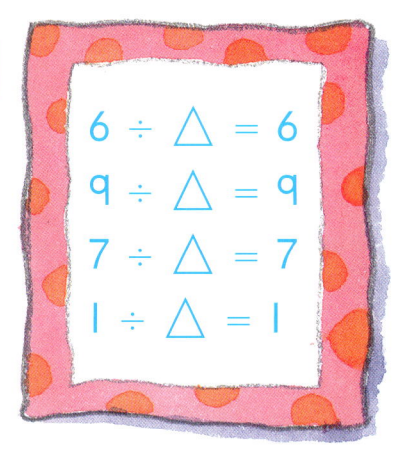

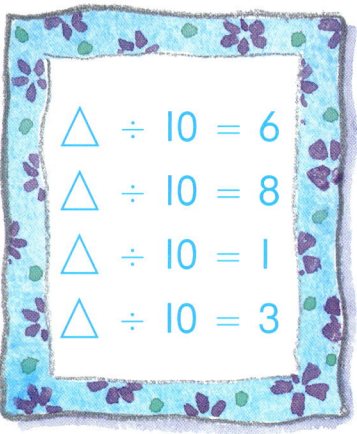

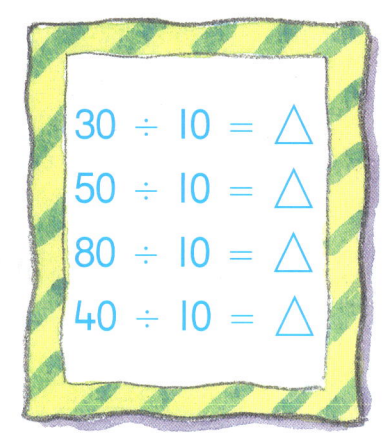

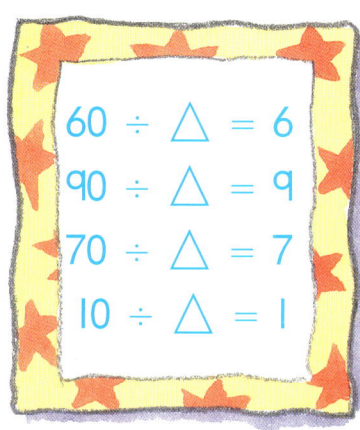

**B1** Copy and complete the number sentences.

a
30 ÷ 1 = △
50 ÷ 1 = △
80 ÷ 1 = △
40 ÷ 1 = △

b
30 ÷ 10 = △
50 ÷ 10 = △
80 ÷ 10 = △
40 ÷ 10 = △

c
6 ÷ △ = 6
9 ÷ △ = 9
7 ÷ △ = 7
1 ÷ △ = 1

d
60 ÷ △ = 6
90 ÷ △ = 9
70 ÷ △ = 7
10 ÷ △ = 1

e
△ ÷ 10 = 6
△ ÷ 10 = 8
△ ÷ 10 = 1
△ ÷ 10 = 3

f
△ ÷ 1 = 60
△ ÷ 1 = 80
△ ÷ 1 = 10
△ ÷ 1 = 30

**C** You can make at least 6 different division sentences with these numbers.

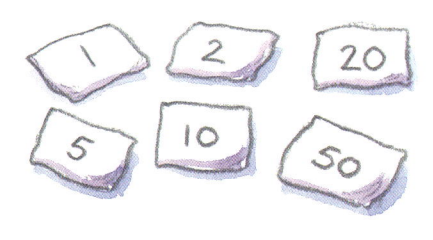

True or false?

1   2   20
5   10   50

| Key idea | When we divide a multiple of 10 by 10, the tens digit moves to become a units digit. |

MD5 Using place value to multiply and divide

# MD5.3 Multiplying by 2, 3, 4 or 5

**Key idea** We can multiply numbers up to 5 by 2, 3, 4 and 5.

**B1** Copy and complete.

3 cars  3 × 4 = ☐ wheels
4 cars  4 × 4 = ☐ wheels
5 cars  5 × 4 = ☐ wheels

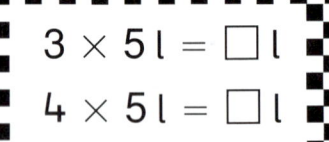

**B2**

a)  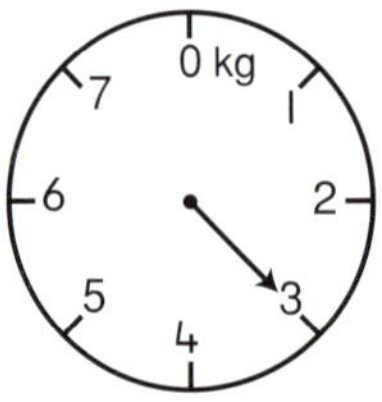
2 weigh  2 × 3 kg = ☐ kg
4 weigh  4 × 3 kg = ☐ kg
5 weigh  5 × 3 kg = ☐ kg

b) 
3 cans  3 × 5 l = ☐ l
4 cans  4 × 5 l = ☐ l
2 cans  2 × 5 l = ☐ l

c) 1 lap is 2 km
5 laps  5 × 2 km = ☐ km
4 laps  4 × 2 km = ☐ km
3 laps  3 × 2 km = ☐ km

d) The Big Race Child ticket £5
5 cost  5 × £5 = £☐
4 cost  4 × £5 = £☐
3 cost  3 × £5 = £☐

# MD5.4 Solving multiplication and division problems

> **Key idea**  We can use multiply and divide to solve problems.

**B1** How many stamps were bought?

Copy and complete the number sentences.

a. Ping spends 50p on 10p stamps   ☐ ÷ 10 = ☐

b. Penny spends 25p on 5p stamps   ☐ ÷ 5 = ☐

c. Peter spends 18p on 2p stamps   ☐ ÷ 2 = ☐

**B2** Susan has only 2p and 5p stamps.

Which stamps can she use to send her letters?

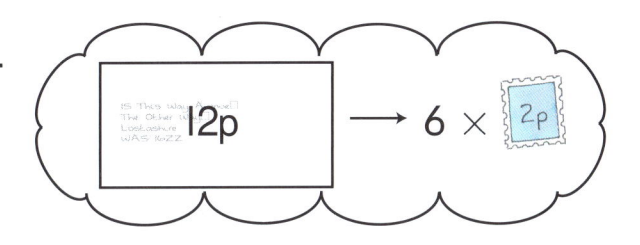

12p → 6 × 2p

a. 15p
b. 20p
c. 14p
d. 25p

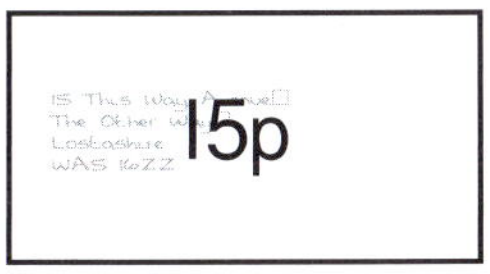

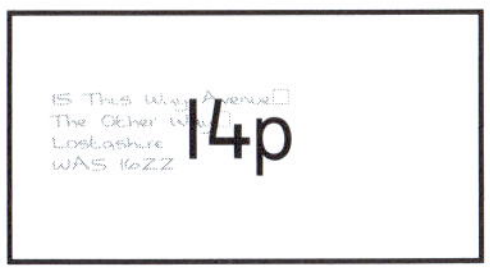

**B3** Find a different way for each letter.

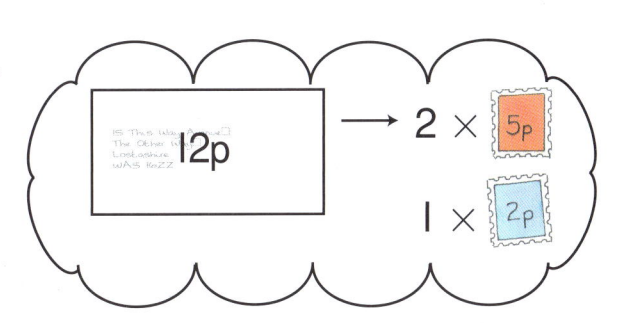

12p → 2 × 5p
    1 × 2p

**C1** There are only 2p and 5p stamps.

Which amounts up to 50p can be made?

1p → no
2p → 1 × 2p
3p → no
4p → 2 × 2p
5p → 1 × 5p

MD5 Using place value to multiply and divide

49

# SP2.2 Add, subtract, multiply or divide

> **Key idea** We can add, subtract, multiply or divide to solve problems.

Jamie 
8 years old

Nandita
12 years old 

Today is Jamie's and Nandita's birthday.

**B** Write your answer and a number sentence for each problem.

**B1** Each got twice as many cards as their age. How many cards for:

a Jamie?      b Nandita?

**B2** How many rows of 4 candles on each cake?

a Jamie      b Nandita

**B3** a How much older is Nandita than Jamie?

b How old will Jamie be in 5 years' time?

c How old was Nandita 3 years ago?

**B4** Jamie's dad is 5 times as old as Jamie. How old is Jamie's dad?

**B5** There are 30 balloons at Jamie's party. Everyone gets 3 balloons. How many people are at the party?

## SP2.3 Using more than 1 operation

> **Key idea** Sometimes we have to use more than 1 operation to solve a problem.

Write your answer and 2 number sentences to show what you did.

**A1** There are 8 people in the shop.
7 more come in and 3 go out.
How many people are there now?

**A2** Mr Khan has 2 shelves and puts 6 boxes of chocolates on each shelf. He sells 3 boxes. How many boxes are left?

**B1** There are 28 cakes in the tray.
Ami buys 13 and Ali buys 7.
How many are left?

**B2** Tom buys a bag of 12 chews. He eats 2 then shares the rest with Bill. How many does Bill get?

**B3** There are 6 orange sweets and 4 lemon sweets in each pack.
How many sweets are in 10 packs?

**C1** In Class 2 there are 3 tables.
8 children sit at each table.
How many boxes does Mrs Crow buy so each child in her class gets a chocolate egg?

**C2** How many boxes would Mrs Crow need if her class sat at:
  **a** 5 tables of 6?   **b** 8 tables of 4?   **c** 7 tables of 4?

SP2 Solving problems

# SP3.1 Using addition and subtraction

| Key idea | We can use + and − to solve word problems. |
|---|---|

**Carlo's ice creams**

| Ice cream | | Extra toppings | |
|---|---|---|---|
| cones | 35p | raspberry sauce | 6p |
| wafers | 40p | chocolate flake | 12p |
| tubs | 45p | mint fudge | 15p |
| | | coloured dips | 9p |

**B1** Write down an ice cream and a topping for each child.

Peter 75p  Jodi 60p  Hannah 50p  Nico 70p

**B2** How much money does each child have left?
Write number sentences to show how you worked it out.

**C1** The twins Ashley and Adam have £1 between them to spend on ice cream.

If they both choose the same ice cream and topping, what could they buy?

Find all their possible choices.

Write number sentences to show how you know.

## SP3.2 Missing numbers

> **Key idea** — We can write a number sentence with a missing number to help us solve a problem.

**B1** Write number sentences to help you solve these problems.

- **a** There are 2 lion cubs on the grass and some in the cave. There are 6 lion cubs altogether. How many cubs are in the cave?

- **b** There were 25 birds. Some flew away. 12 birds are left. How many birds flew away?

- **c** This morning there were some penguins in the pool. Now there are 5 times as many. If there are 20 penguins now, how many were there this morning?

- **d** The zoo keeper shares bananas between 5 monkeys. They each get 3 bananas. How many bananas did the zookeeper have?

**B2** The bears have walked over some signs and numbers. Work out the missing signs and numbers, and write the number sentences.

- **a** 14 🐾 🐾 = 22
- **b** 28 🐾 🐾 = 22
- **c** 29 🐾 🐾 = 39
- **d** 35 🐾 🐾 = 29
- **e** 10 🐾 🐾 = 40
- **f** 5 🐾 🐾 = 15
- **g** 8 🐾 🐾 = 4
- **h** 30 🐾 🐾 = 10

**C1** Write zoo number stories to match some of the bear paw number sentences.

SP3 Solving problems

## SP3.3 Choosing operations

> **Key idea**: We can use +, −, × and ÷ to solve money problems.

**A1** You have 14p in your purse.
How much will you have when:

a  you have 7p more?
b  you double your money?
c  you spend half your money?
d  you have 8p more?
e  your mum gives you £1?
f  you buy 3 sweets at 4p each?

**B1** Work out how much each customer spends at the DIY store.

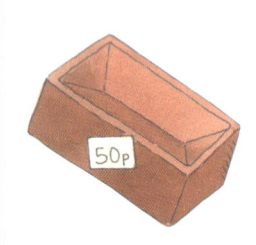

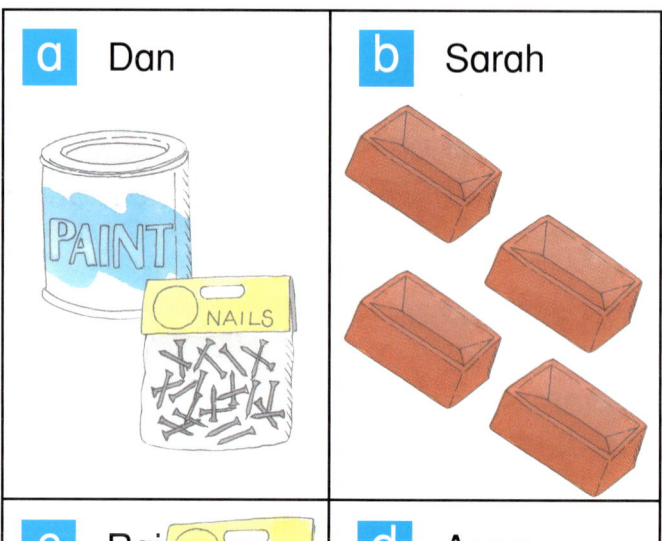

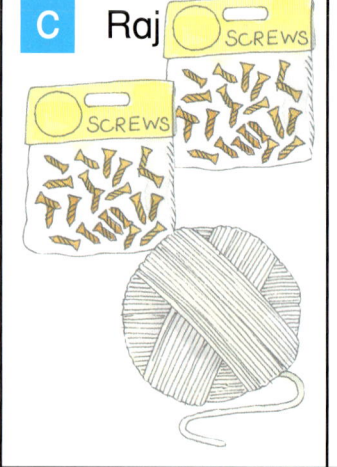

a Dan — PAINT, NAILS
b Sarah — 4 bricks
c Raj — 2 bags of SCREWS, ball of string
d Anna — hammer, NAILS

Prices shown: string 40p, screws 31p, brick 50p, paint £2·50, nails 25p, paint brush 49p, hammer 75p

**B2** Pete buys 2 paint brushes. What is his change from £1?

54  SP3 Solving problems

# M4.3 Solving weight problems

> **Key idea** We can use what we know about numbers and measures to solve problems.

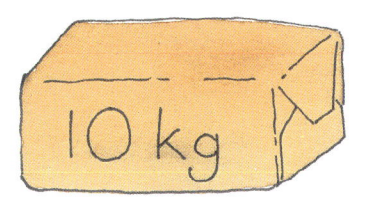

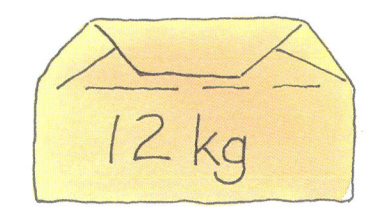

Parcels: 10 kg, 12 kg, 5 kg

★1  a  Which parcel is the heaviest?
    b  Which parcel is the lightest?

★2  How much do the 3 parcels weigh altogether?

★3  What is the difference between the heaviest and lightest parcels?

A1  What is the hidden weight on each parcel?

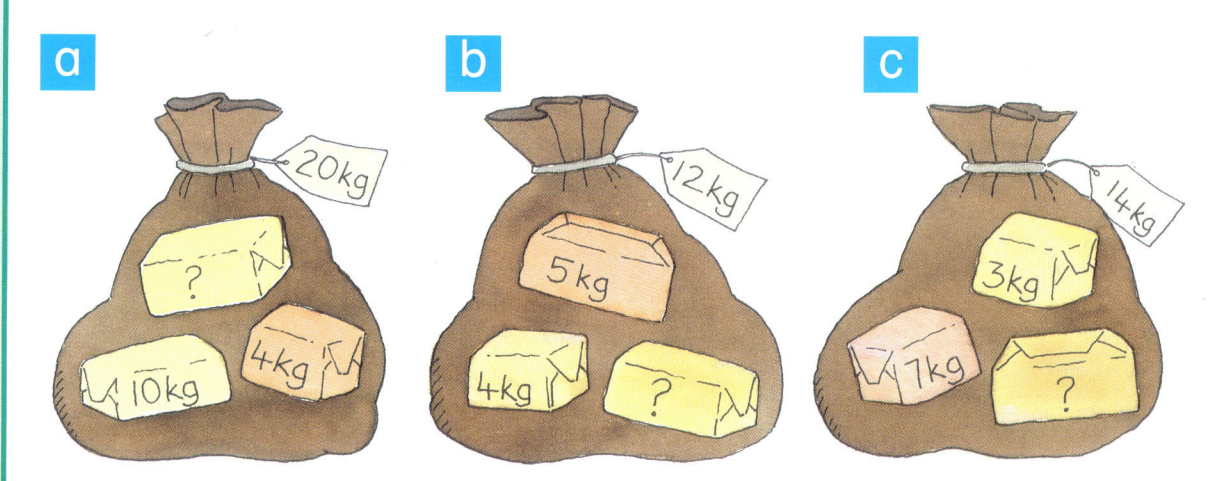

a  Sack 20 kg: contains ?, 10 kg, 4 kg
b  Sack 12 kg: contains 5 kg, 4 kg, ?
c  Sack 14 kg: contains 3 kg, 7 kg, ?

A2  What is the total weight of the 3 sacks?

M4 Solving measures problems

55

**B1** How much does it cost to send parcel I abroad?

**B2** It cost Jake £14 to send a parcel inland.
How heavy was his parcel?

**B3** What is the total cost of sending parcels E and F inland?

**B4** How much more does it cost to send parcel I abroad than parcel F?

**B5** Tanya paid £18. She sent 2 parcels inland. Which 2 might she have sent?

**C** Put 3 parcels in each sack so that each sack weighs 10 kg in total. Use parcels A–I above.

Use digit cards.
Put the heaviest parcels in each first.

**Key idea** We can use what we know about numbers and measures to solve problems.

M4 Solving measures problems

# M6.2 Multiplying and dividing capacities

> **Key idea**  We can use what we know about multiplying and dividing to solve problems involving capacity.

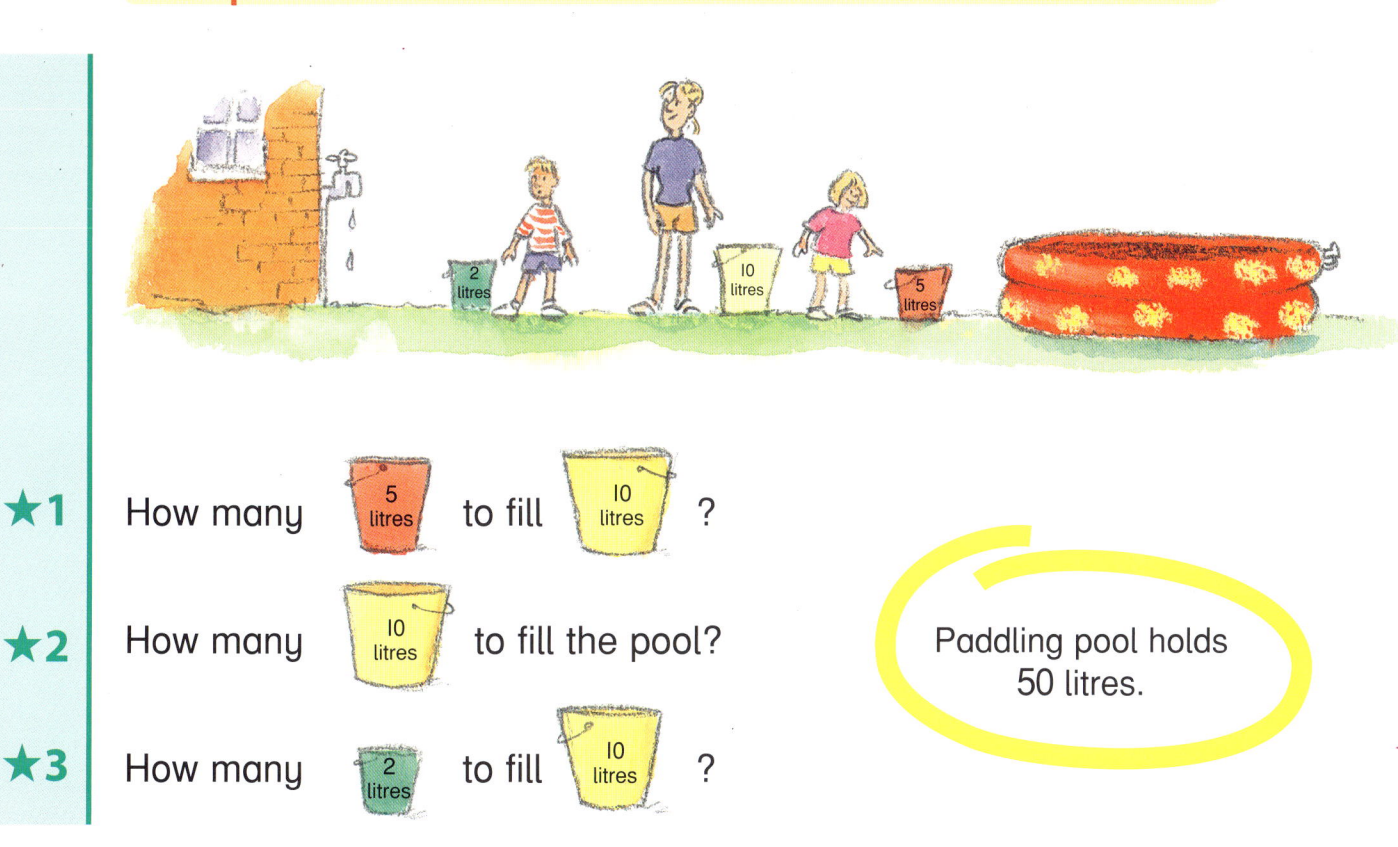

★1 How many 5 litres to fill 10 litres?

★2 How many 10 litres to fill the pool?

★3 How many 2 litres to fill 10 litres?

*Paddling pool holds 50 litres.*

**A1** Mum puts four 10-litre bucketfuls into the pool. How much water is in the pool?

**A2** How many 5-litre bucketfuls will fill the pool?

**A3** How many 2-litre bucketfuls will fill the pool?

**B1** Find 3 different ways to fill the pool. Use all 3 buckets each time.

**C1** Each person puts 2 bucketfuls into the pool. How many more litres altogether do they need to fill the pool?

**C2** How can they do this? Find different ways.

M6 Solving capacity problems

# M6.3 Solving capacity problems

| Key idea | We can use what we know about numbers and measures to solve problems about capacity. |

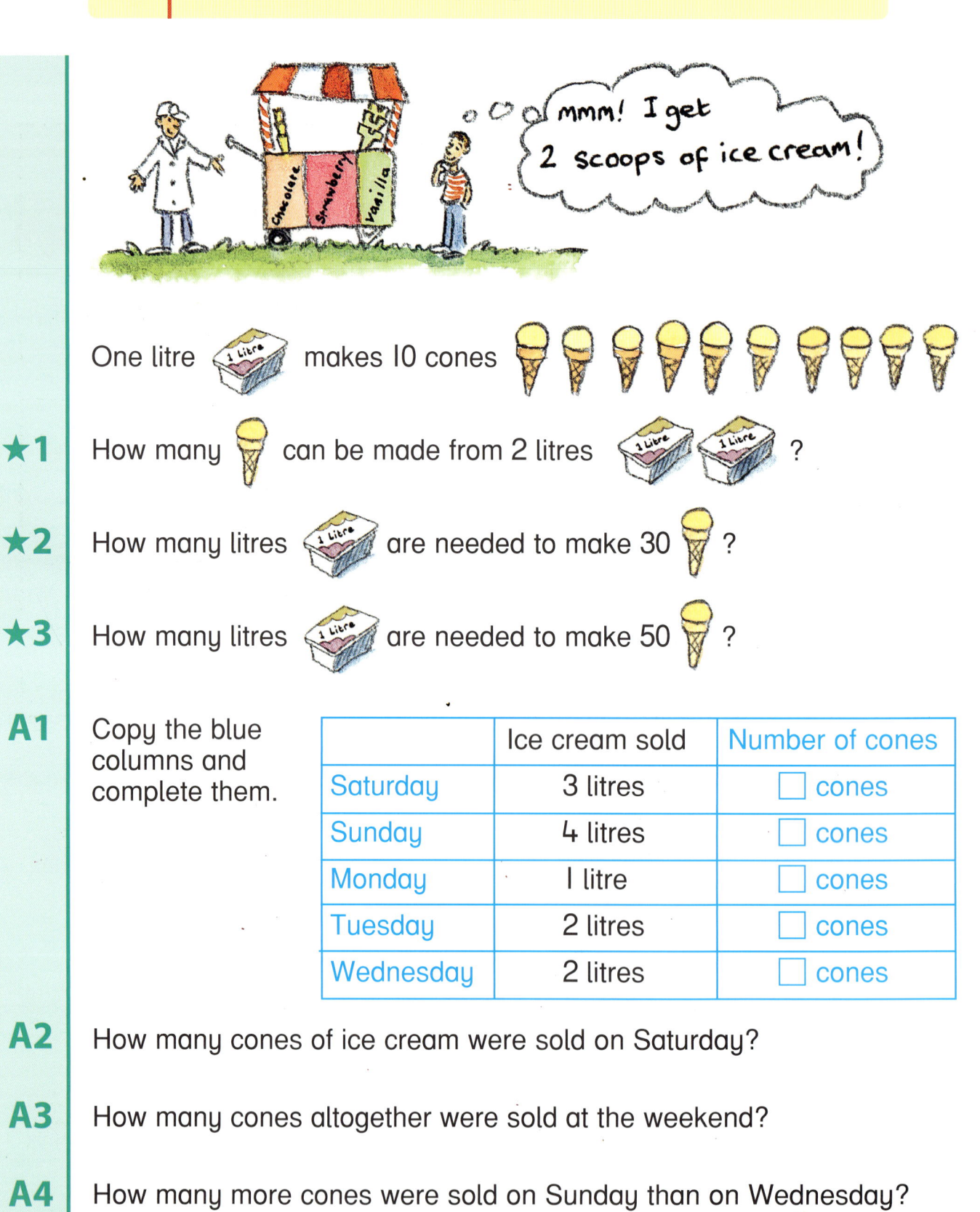

One litre makes 10 cones

★1  How many 🍦 can be made from 2 litres ?

★2  How many litres are needed to make 30 🍦 ?

★3  How many litres are needed to make 50 🍦 ?

A1  Copy the blue columns and complete them.

|  | Ice cream sold | Number of cones |
|---|---|---|
| Saturday | 3 litres | ☐ cones |
| Sunday | 4 litres | ☐ cones |
| Monday | 1 litre | ☐ cones |
| Tuesday | 2 litres | ☐ cones |
| Wednesday | 2 litres | ☐ cones |

A2  How many cones of ice cream were sold on Saturday?

A3  How many cones altogether were sold at the weekend?

A4  How many more cones were sold on Sunday than on Wednesday?

58    M6 Solving capacity problems

# M7.4 Quarter to

> **Key idea** Quarter to is the same as 15 minutes to the next hour.

**B** What time is it? Write the digital times.

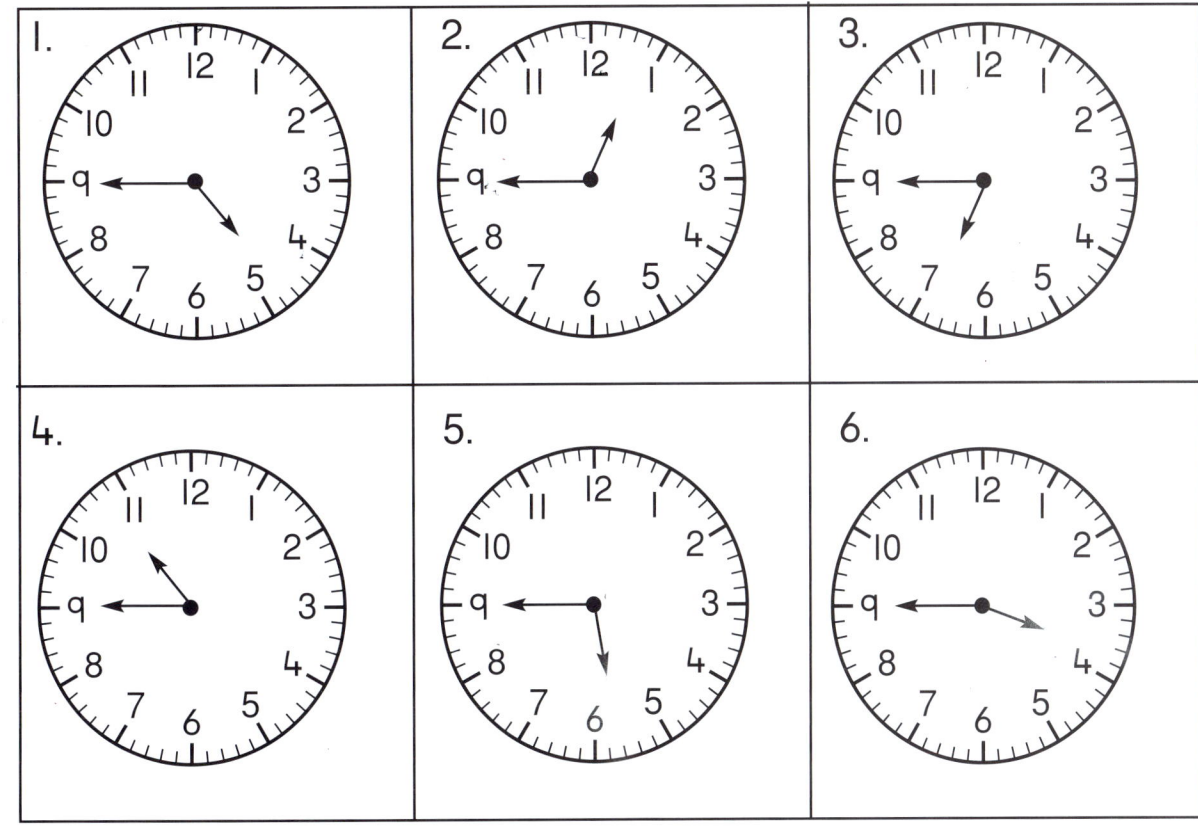

1. 
2. 
3. 
4. 
5. 
6. 

7. quarter to 7

8. quarter to 9

9. quarter to 3

M7 Time

59

# M7.6 Time problems 2

| Key idea | We can use what we know about counting and number bonds to solve time problems. |

|  | Start time | Slide pool | Big pool | Finish time |
|---|---|---|---|---|
| Gita | 10:30 | 15 minutes | C1 | 11:15 |
| Anjay | C2 : | half an hour | 45 minutes | 1:15 |
| Sophie | 4:15 | C3 | 1 hour | 6:00 |
| Luke | 1:30 | 2 hours | C4 | 3:45 |
| Toby | C5 : | 2 hours | 30 minutes | 11:15 |

Use the table to answer the questions.

**C1** How long did Gita spend in the big pool?

**C2** What time did Anjay start?

**C3** How long did Sophie spend in the slide pool?

**C4** How long did Luke spend in the big pool?

**C5** What time did Toby start?

## SS2.4 Solving shape problems

> Key idea: We can use what we know about shapes to investigate and solve problems.

**A3** Make these skeleton shapes from straws.

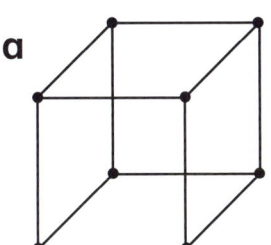

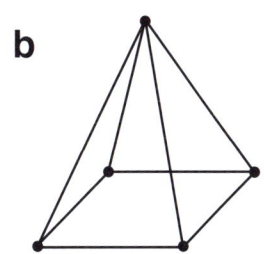

a   b

How many edges and corners does each shape have?

How many straws did you use to make each shape?

**A4** Can you make this shape from straws?

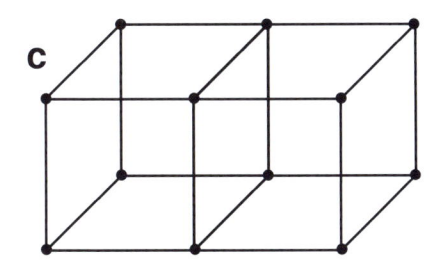

c

How many straws did you use?

How many more straws than shape **a**?

**B1** Now make this shape.

How many straws did you use?

How many more straws than shape **c**?

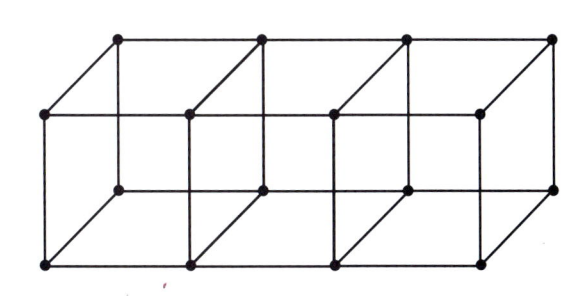

**B2** How many straws would you need to make a shape with 4 cubes?

**B3** How many straws would you need to make a shape with 5 cubes?

SS2 3-D shapes

# SS3.2 A line of symmetry

> **Key idea** If a pattern has a line of symmetry then it is symmetrical.

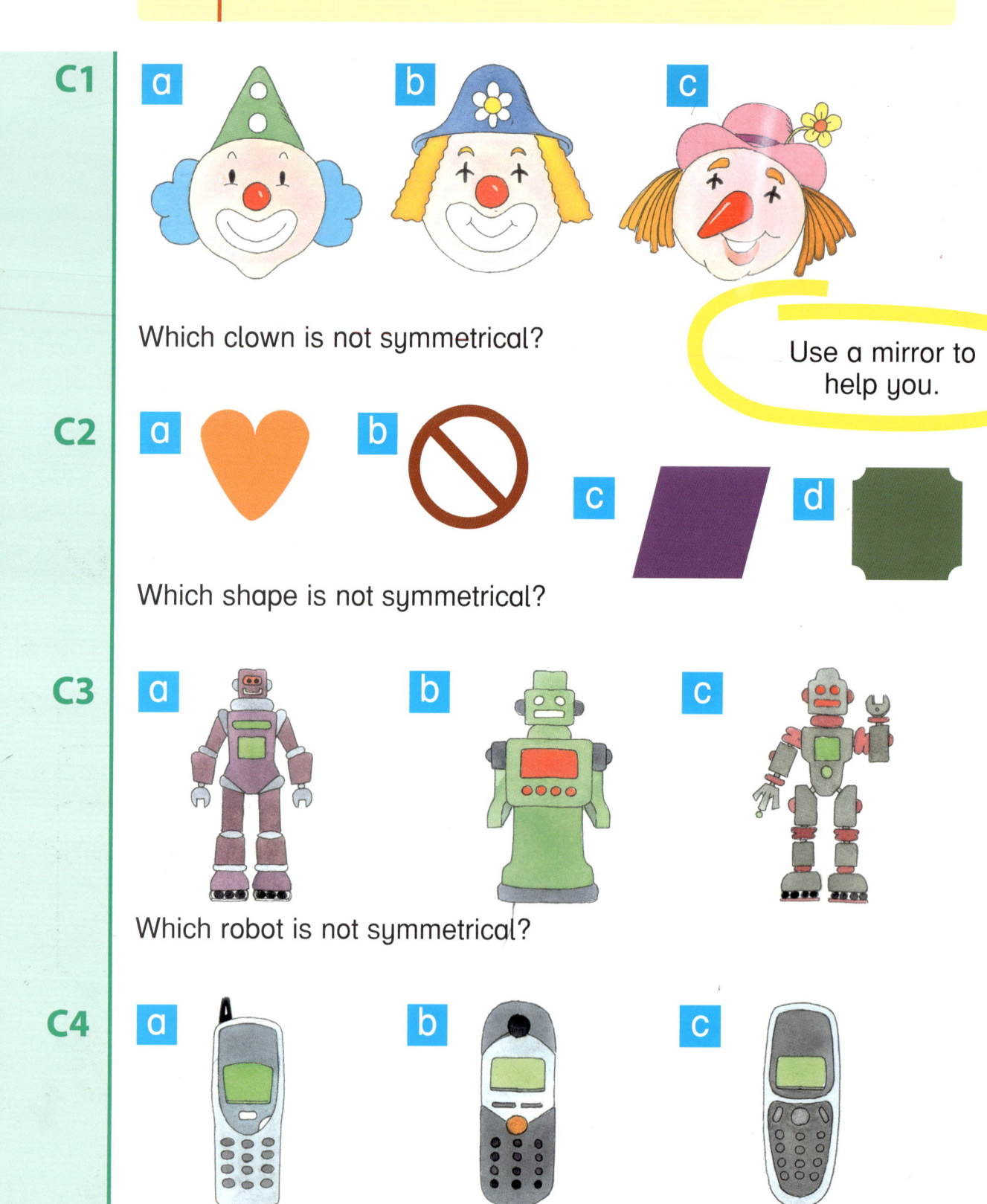

**C1** a  b  c

Which clown is not symmetrical?

*Use a mirror to help you.*

**C2** a  b  c  d

Which shape is not symmetrical?

**C3** a  b  c

Which robot is not symmetrical?

**C4** a  b  c

Which mobile phone is not symmetrical?

SS3 Line symmetry

# SS3.3 Making symmetrical patterns

| Key idea | Try to make the parts on either side of a line of symmetry match exactly. |
|---|---|

**B3** Draw and cut out two shapes like this.
Use them to make a symmetrical shape.
Draw it. Put on the line of symmetry.

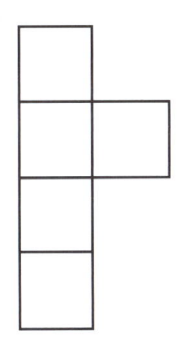

**C1** Use a mirror to read these words.

HIDE    BIKE

RICE    CHICK

**C2** Copy this pattern.

- Colour 1 more square to make it symmetrical.
- Add 2 red squares
  2 yellow squares
  2 green squares
  to make your own symmetrical pattern.

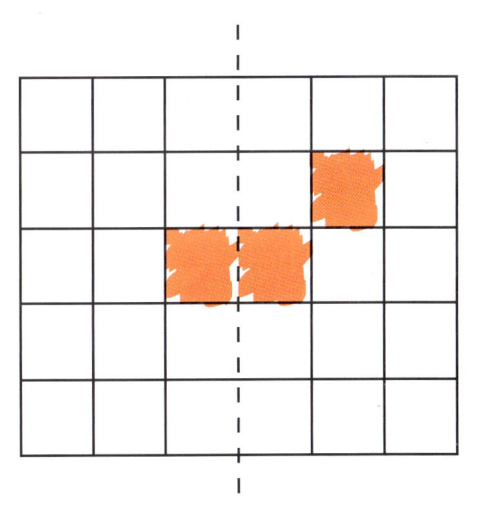

**C3** Use a mirror.

Place it so that you can see only 1 ladybird.

Move it to see 2, 3, 4, 5, 6 ladybirds.

SS3 Line symmetry

## SS4.1 Where is it?

> **Key idea** We can say where something is with a position word.

**B**

on top of · in · underneath · next to · above · beside · in the middle of

Write these sentences in your book and complete them.

1. The 🫗 is _____ the table.
2. The 🟡 is _____ the chair.
3. The 🪑 is _____ the table.
4. The 🐈 is _____ the table.
5. The 🍎 is _____ the 🥣 , _____ the 🫗 .
6. The 🪵 is _____ the 🐈 and _____ the 🫗 .
7. The 🥣 is _____ the 🍎 .
8. The ⚽ is _____ the 🐈 , _____ the 🪵 .

**C**

Get 3 objects. Give your partner the same objects.
Set out the objects on the table.
Describe their position to your partner for them to copy.
Do they put the objects in the same position?
Now try with 4 or 5 objects.

64  SS4 Position and direction

## SS4.2 Routes

> **Key idea** — We can draw and follow routes on squared paper.

**START**

Follow the directions. Begin at 'START'. Where do you finish?

★1   **a** Up 2 squares.
        Across right 2 squares.

   **b** Up 3 squares.
        Across right 4 squares.

A1   **a** Up 1 square.
        Across right 3 squares.
        Up 4 squares.

   **b** Across right 3 squares.
        Up 4 squares.
        Across left 2 squares.

B1   Write directions to get to **a** and **b**.

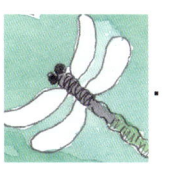

C1   Put a counter on a square you choose. Give your friend directions to it.

SS4 Position and direction

65

## SS4.3 Clockwise or anti-clockwise?

| Key idea | We can move clockwise and anti-clockwise. |

**A1**

Follow Primesh's route.
Which way did he turn at each corner?
Write a list like this:
1 – clockwise
2 – clockwise
3 –

## SS5.1 Right angles

> **Key idea** | A right angle is a quarter turn.

**B1** Look at the picture below.
Use a right angle tester to find the right angles.
How many can you find?

**B2** Which shapes have right angles at all their corners?
Can you name them?

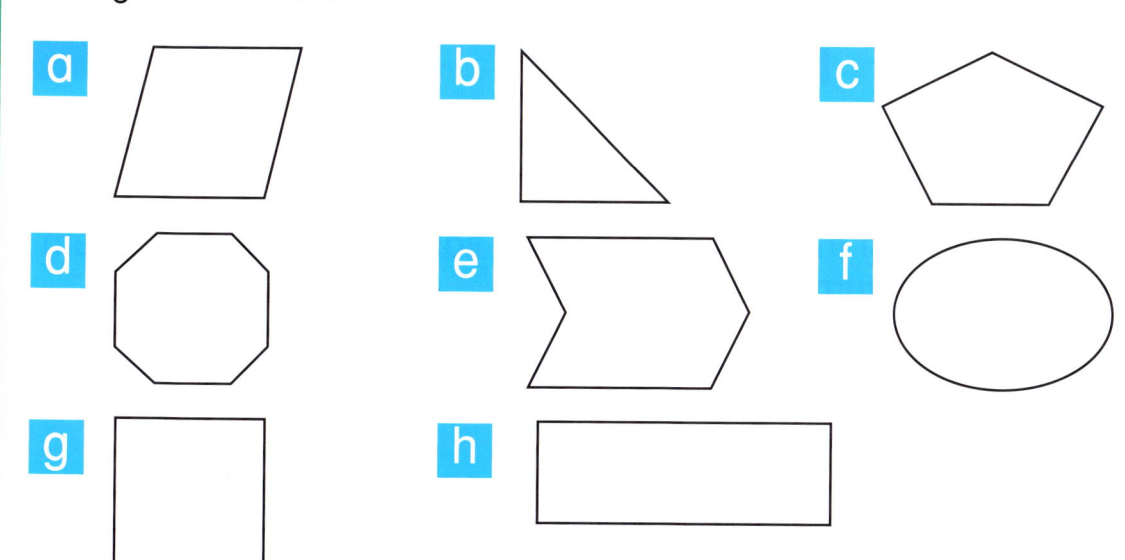

a  b  c
d  e  f
g  h

**B3** Use your right angle tester to find 5 right angles in the classroom.
Draw them.

SS5 Movement and angle

67

**B1** Look at the pictogram.

- **a** How many yellow shapes?
- **b** How many more blue than yellow shapes?
- **c** What is the most common colour?
- **d** What is the least common colour?

**Colours in Ali's pattern**

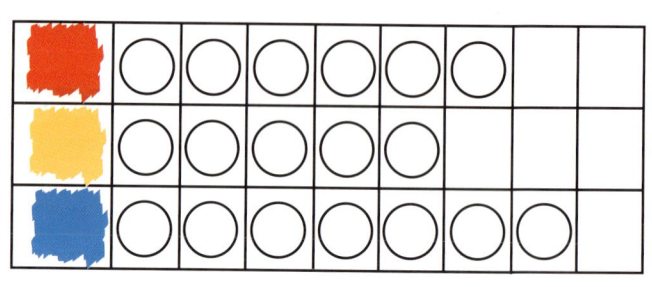

○ represents 1 shape

**B2** Write 2 questions about the pictogram in B1.

**C1**
- **a** Make a pictogram from this information:

**How much pocket money each week?**

| Less than £1 | £1 exactly | More than £1 |
|---|---|---|
| Jo    Tom<br>Esme    Ali<br>Chloe    Donna | Emma  Heather<br>Bilal    Natalie<br>Ahmed    Jack<br>Charlie    Angel<br>Danny | Ben<br>Lauren<br>Imran<br>Kate |

Remember to write a title.

- **b** How much pocket money is most common?
- **c** Do more children have more than £1 or less than £1?

**C2**
- **a** Find out how many clubs your friends go to each week.
- **b** Sort the data into 3 sets.
- **c** Talk to your partner. Did they make the same sets?

I've chosen less than 2, 2 exactly, more than 2.

**Key idea** We can read a pictogram and answer questions.

70  HD2 Pictograms

# HD3.1 Block graphs

> **Key idea** We can draw a block graph to show information.

# HD3.2 Reading block graphs

> **Key idea** We can read a block graph and answer questions.

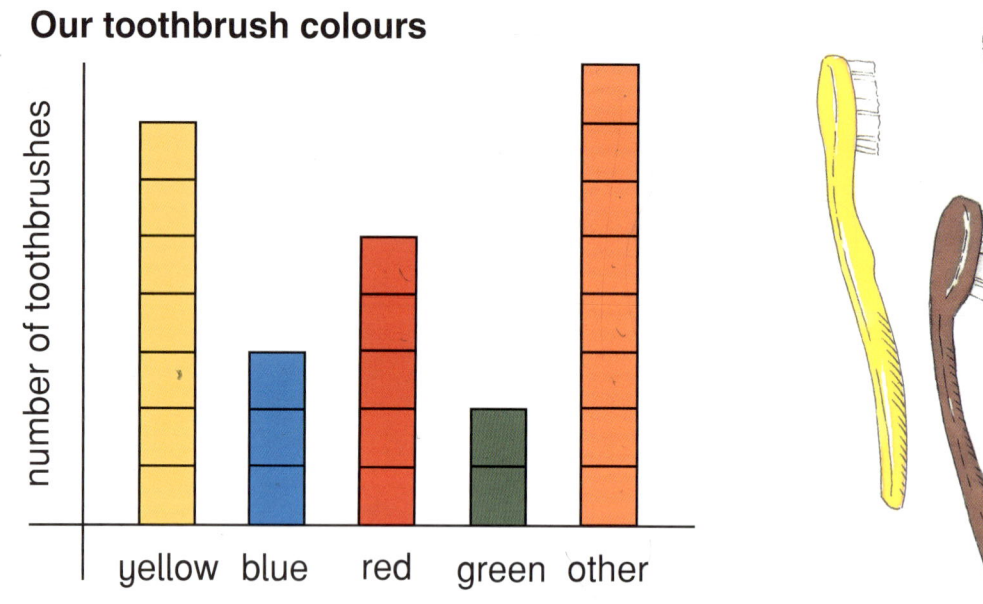

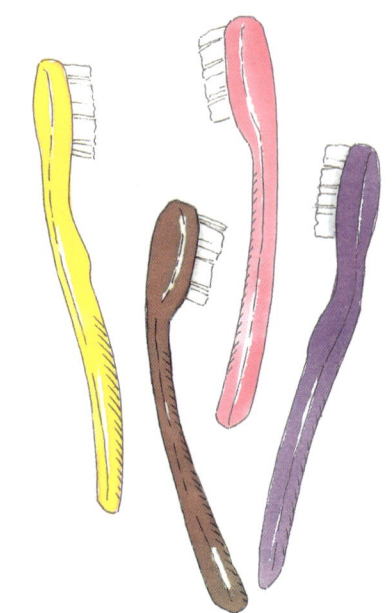

**A** **Our toothbrush colours**

number of toothbrushes

yellow | blue | red | green | other

**B** You need question cards B1–B7 and a partner.
- Look at the graph.
- Talk about questions B1–B7 and then answer them.

**Our shoe sizes**

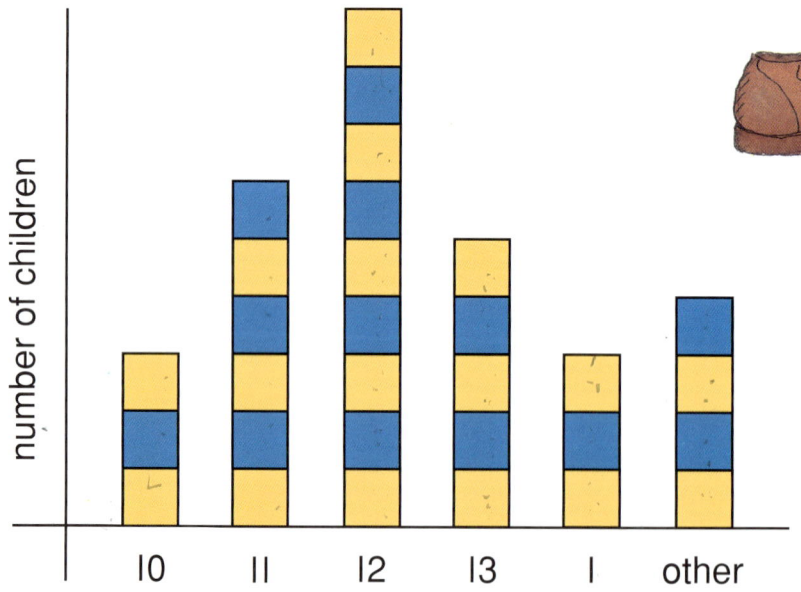

number of children

10 | 11 | 12 | 13 | 1 | other

**C** Do question cards C1 and C2 for the block graph in A.

HD3 Block graphs

AS 83